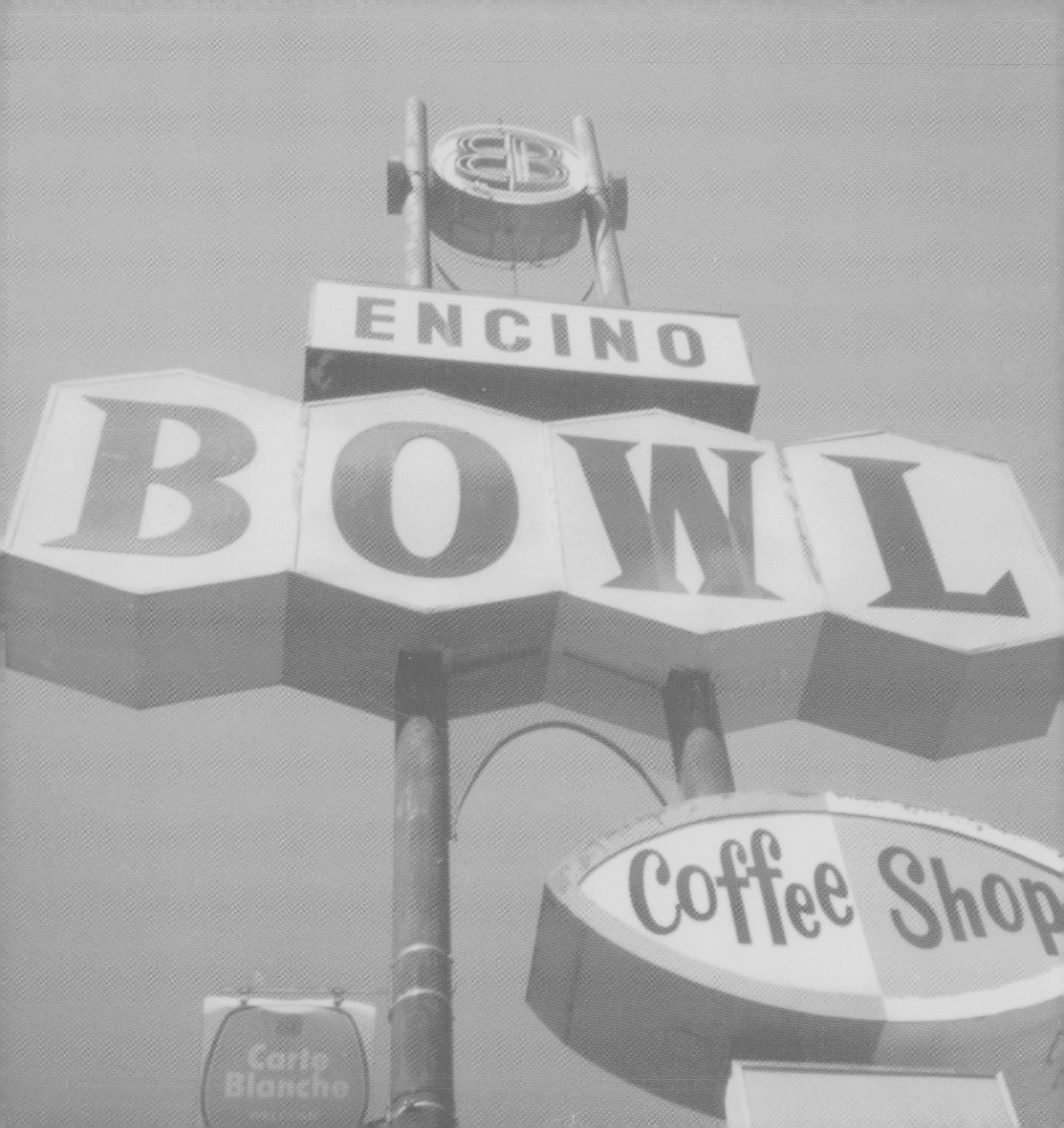
ENCINO
BOWL
Coffee Shop
Carte Blanche

HAL LIFSON'S
1966!

A PERSONAL VIEW OF
THE COOLEST YEAR IN
POP CULTURE HISTORY

BY HAL LIFSON

FOREWORD BY ADAM WEST
INTRODUCTION BY NANCY SINATRA

bonus books

Chicago and Los Angeles

Book Design: lorenz co., Los Angeles
Front Cover Design: Mark London
Editor: Devon Freeny
Production Manager: Keith Barrows

Publisher: Jeffrey A. Stern

06 05 04 03 02   5 4 3 2 1

Library of Congress Control Number 2002108947

ISBN 1-56625-182-6

Bonus Books
160 E. Illinois St.
Chicago, IL 60611

Manufactured in Singapore

To my parents, Francene and Jerry. Thank you for all your love and guidance—and for letting me play the drums despite the neighbors' objections.

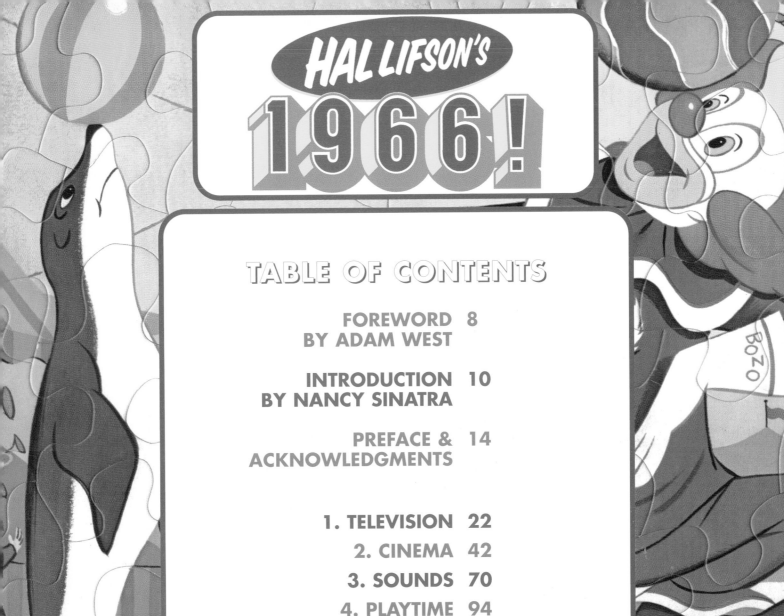

HAL LIFSON'S 1966!

TABLE OF CONTENTS

FOREWORD 8
BY ADAM WEST

INTRODUCTION 10
BY NANCY SINATRA

PREFACE & 14
ACKNOWLEDGMENTS

1. TELEVISION 22
2. CINEMA 42
3. SOUNDS 70
4. PLAYTIME 94
5. READING 110
6. FASHION 132
7. FOOD & DRINK 150
8. ON THE GO 170
9. FACES & PLACES 186

I'm delighted to introduce Hal Lifson's guide to 1966, a milestone year in American pop culture. Among many significant events of this year, both political and cultural: Nancy Sinatra's hit "These Boots Are Made for Walkin'" became an anthem; Ronald Reagan entered politics on a grand scale as governor of California; my friends Steve McQueen and Dean Martin were finding success on the silver screen; and the entire country was caught up in the "3 Bs"—Bond, Beatles, and *Batman*, which premiered January 12, 1966.

As Hal will impress upon you, 1966 was indeed a wonderful year for new ideas and creative expression. *Batman* premiered in the right place at the right time and the show became an instant smash. The *Batman* theme would be recorded by at least eight different artists, and yours truly (no Fred Astaire or Gene Kelly) inspired a national dance craze called—what else?—the Batusi!

You'll enjoy reading Hal Lifson's perspective on one of the most engrossing and fun years of the twentieth century. Filled with rare photos and unique anecdotes, this book promises to take you on a terrific trip to Hal's favorite place.

Hal's journey into American pop culture is a loving tribute to the more joyful side of the '60s. Enjoy!

In 1966, a young boy with a grape Kool-Aid mustache sat cross-legged in front of the family television set and watched me perform on *The Ed Sullivan Show*. He lived in the San Fernando Valley, and was already developing a deep attachment to the suburban culture of boulevards, drive-in movies, and themed restaurants. His was a happy childhood of Schwinn bikes, *Archie* comics, and Bob's Big Boy, and he soaked it all up like a human Scott towel. His name was Hal Lifson.

Many years later, in May 1994, Hal Lifson was working as a creative consultant at Rhino Records, the label that had produced my two "greatest hits" collections. He sent me an enthusiastic fax in which he expressed his respect for my music and announced that he'd like to see my original albums reissued on CD. While raising my kids, I had put aside my musical aspirations, but Hal's interest helped me to realize how much I missed this part of my life. Before I knew it, he had begun working for me as my manager and media strategist.

In nearly three decades, Hal's passion for the popular culture of the 1960s had not dwindled. He was especially interested in the nostalgic details of my career, and he applied what he learned toward his marketing efforts. His hard work and enthusiasm paid off in 1995, when four of my early albums were rereleased on the Sundazed label, followed by my first solo album in over twenty years, *One More Time*. In 1996, three more albums were reissued, and in the next few years Hal and I worked on several compilation packages as well. We embarked on a pretty intensive promotional campaign that included a layout in a 1995 issue of *Playboy*, and a sellout show at the House of Blues.

Over the past eight years, Hal has done an excellent job booking concert dates around the country. The popular show *Sex and the City* used "These Boots Are Made for Walkin'" in a January 2002 episode. My new album

California Girl was released in April 2002 on Disney's Buena Vista label. Hal has truly been the architect of my recent career. He helped me get back into my music, and for that I owe him a debt of gratitude.

I am also grateful to have had the opportunity to share in Hal's affection for an era that was historically and creatively rich. Hal's love of the '60s became a valuable tool in his work as a writer and promoter, but it never stopped being a source of childlike wonder as well. Not only does he know the title and release date of every hit song from 1966, but he can also describe the smell of Prell shampoo, and the subtle difference in taste between 7-Up and Bubble Up (whether you care to know or not!). And should you want to see an original Fresca bottle, or a vintage *Mary Poppins* lunchbox, you will surely find it in Hal's collection. Spontaneously, Hal throws out questions like, "Do you prefer an Oreo or Hydrox? The Beach Boys or the Monkees? Betty or Veronica?" He still chews Chiclets gum, prefers York Peppermint Patties to Junior Mints—and don't get him started on the chips and salsa from the retro landmark Casa Vega! This love for all things 1966 resonates throughout his professional and personal life. It is his art form.

In this book, Hal's art has found tangible expression. He has at last created an outlet through which to share rare images from his extensive memorabilia collections, his encyclopedic knowledge of '60s culture, and his wonderfully unique perspective on what is generally considered a highly charged era. *Hal Lifson's 1966!* is dedicated to all the cool things he remembers from his childhood, and it shows how his life and career were shaped by his longing for those days of innocence.

While Hal was enjoying life as a child in the 1960s, I had a very different experience. To me, the '60s was a decade of confusion and change, achievement and expression. Our beloved, visionary president John F. Kennedy was brutally taken from us, as were Robert Kennedy and civil rights leader Martin Luther King. Our society was rapidly shifting as a result of internal strife and international unrest; drugs were prolific; and the birth control pill changed behavior and relationships. We were a nation torn by a war most of us resented and in which an entire generation was involved, either enlisting, protesting, or running away to Canada to avoid being drafted.

Perhaps as a reaction to the national and international political turmoil, it all seemed to come together creatively. Hal once sent me an article from the *Los Angeles Times* by rock music critic Roger Catlin, which proclaimed 1966 the best year of rock music (as if I needed convincing). For me personally, 1966 was nothing short of a spectacular year: a number-one record, several top ten songs, albums, television shows, movies, an appearance with my dad on *A Man and His Music Part II*. Nineteen sixty-six represented a dichotomy of social troubles and creative triumphs.

Six-year-old Hal was only aware of the triumphs. He saw only the colorful and creative aspects of this year—the music, movies, fashion, toys, and more. It is these joyous memories that shine through in everything he says and writes. Hal never loses sight of the truths that lead us to the people and things we hold dear. He cherishes them and is driven by them. That kind of passion is rare, indeed. I hope you find *Hal Lifson's 1966!* as entertaining and inspiring as I do.

And, Hal: thanks for asking me to write this introduction, proving once again that no good deed shall go unpublished.

I have always believed that the 1960s were by far the most creative and influential decade of the twentieth century. The culture of the period changed the world in many different ways, and much of this change was progressive, a sign of the new generation that was coming into power in the post–World War II years. While many books have been written about different aspects of the 1960s, I know of no author who has attempted to single out the very best year for popular culture in the '60s, and, in doing so, proposed a "mascot" year for the whole decade.

With this book, I have done just that. In the following pages, I will illustrate why I believe that 1966 is the definitive year of the '60s. But *1966!* is not a scholarly history, nor is it an encyclopedia encompassing every cultural element of the year. Instead, it is a scrapbook of all my favorite things from this very special year, because the best way for me to demonstrate the cultural impact of 1966 is to show the profound influence it had on *my* life.

I was born on July 16, 1960, seven months into the new decade. The first several years of my life were spent with my mom and dad and little brother Bobby, who joined us in 1962, at our pad in the Los Angeles suburb of Encino. We lived in a white house with black trim on the window boxes and coral rocks on the roof. Our house had a circular driveway and a walnut tree in front. In the backyard was a lava-rock waterfall that only worked for a few years—but even afterwards my buddies and I had fun climbing on it, using it as the Batcave or for GI Joe training missions. I remember filling our canteens with Tang for extra stamina in the wilderness.

In January of 1966, I began my second semester of kindergarten at Hesby Street Elementary School, and in the fall I entered first grade. My sister Byrdie was born in March, one of the many momentous events of the year.

Although I was only five and six years old during 1966, I was mesmerized by all forms of entertainment. I listened to music constantly on my transistor radio, and I can still recall the thrill of hearing the new Beatles singles "Paperback Writer" and "Rain." With my striped, flared pants and little plastic doctor's bag, I was the hit of the playground. Those candy pills were way out, man!

Television was at a creative peak in '66. I had witnessed the incredible promotional campaign for the launch of the *Batman* TV series in the winter of '65, and I awaited the debut episode on January 12, 1966, with the kind of anticipation that would not reenter my life until 1976—when I obtained my driver's license. Other super-cool TV shows that debuted in '66 and kept me glued to the screen included *The Monkees, T.H.E. Cat, The Green Hornet,* and *Family Affair. The Addams Family* and *The Munsters* aired their last original episodes in early '66, as did *Gidget,* a very well-written and sentimental program starring Sally Field. One of the most endearing romantic shows that premiered in '66 was *That Girl* with Marlo Thomas. Marlo played actress Ann Marie, and to me she was both a fantasy girlfriend and a big-sister figure.

I was so heavily influenced by these shows that I insisted my mom order me the deluxe Batman costume (made of real fabric!) from the Sears catalog. (My brother had the Superman suit and I was always amused at the disclaimer inside the shirt which read, "Remember . . . only Superman can fly.") I even started wearing those big, wide belts with the buckle pushed over to the side, like Peter Tork did on *The Monkees.*

A lot of teenagers lived in our neighborhood, and they congregated in our front yard, especially during the summer months—which, in the Valley, comprised half the year. Our neighbor Marvin Margolies disassembled his family's backyard swing set and sawed off the metal poles to create a basketball backboard frame, which he installed over our garage door. It was amazingly sturdy, and it stands to this day. (Though several years ago I updated it with a Lucite backboard.)

During the summer of '66, the neighborhood teens would play hour after hour of competitive basketball on my family's driveway, which was one of the flattest and smoothest in the neighborhood. I was usually relegated to the role of "Kool-Aid boy," and forced to "hang out" with the chick clique on the sidelines, watching the big guys play. It was kind of difficult for me to make a big impression on these gals, as many of them doubled as my babysitters. From this hip crowd, I learned so much about life, romance, and which were the best attractions to see at Disneyland.

One of my most significant mentors during this year and throughout the '60s was my neighbor David Cohen, known affectionately as "Big Dave." Dave introduced me to sophisticated trends like James Bond movies (*Thunderball* was in the theaters in early '66), *The Man From U.N.C.L.E.*, and the importance of wearing *Playboy* rabbit cufflinks. Along with Adam West on *Batman*, Dave taught me the value of eating healthy; I remember watching TV in his room while he ate a huge salad out of a big plastic lettuce crisper. I was so impressed that he would dump a whole can of Del Monte green beans into his salad, and drink a huge glass of milk out of the tall antique-car tumblers they were giving away up at the corner gas station. Dave was always a respected authority figure in the neighborhood—especially when he began his karate lessons at Chuck Norris's studio in nearby Sherman Oaks.

Sixty-six was the first year that I truly understood the influence that the entertainment industry would have on my life. I developed an interest in playing the drums which has lasted to this day when I began taking lessons this year at the Beechler music store. I coveted the tiger-skin-finish drum set in the window, and I practiced diligently in hopes that my parents would get it for me. Luckily, my dad was a drummer, so he was able to help me learn the basic techniques to get my rock music career off to a great start. I even got my hair cut at a trendy, Carnaby Street–style salon for kids called "Moppets." The barber chair was on top of a big toy bass drum, which I thought was very Warhol. I remember my uncontainable excitement when I got my first real set of drums late in this year. I was determined to become the next Ringo Starr—or, at the very least, Micky Dolenz.

The entertainment of 1966 did not just shape my own life; it transformed the entire world. Standout albums like the Beach Boys' *Pet Sounds*, classic games like Twister, and landmark television series like *Batman* have remained precious to me throughout my life, but they've also become widely recognized as timeless cultural treasures. For this reason, 1966 has always been the high point by which I evaluate all pop culture, and probably the one year that I have chronicled the most passionately in all my years of memorabilia collecting, and all my work as a personal manager, publicist, and radio host. (I was the first deejay in many years to play the extended catalogs of groups like Love, the Zombies, and Booker T. and the MGs on L.A. radio airwaves.)

In the mid 1980s, a few years after I graduated from college, I began to intensely collect all things 1960s—record albums, toys, magazines, and food product advertising. I had saved a few things from my childhood, but, for the most part, I had spent the '70s and early '80s pretty retro-free. I began buying collectibles through a magazine called *Goldmine*, in which different collectors took out ads to sell their treasured items, before eBay existed. I would run ads announcing that I was looking for specific things, like *Batman*, *Green Hornet*, and *Honey West* collectibles. Or even really obscure requests, like when I tried to find my lost Wham-O Water Wiggle again.

I decided to put this book together at the urging of my friend Nancy Sinatra, who felt my fairly massive gallery of '60s memorabilia and my knowledge of the era would be of great interest to many baby boomers—and to '60s enthusiasts of all ages. Now that all my images and thoughts are laid down in this book, I can see more clearly than ever how much 1966 had to offer the world with its strong sense of design and powerful creative expressions. I can see, too, why I loved it so much. For me, the power of this one year is like no other, and I am so thankful that my publisher and friend Jeff Stern believed in my vision enough to let it shine through, unfiltered by conventional marketing concepts that predominate in so many retro-themed projects. I wanted this book to reflect my personal tastes and preferences, so the impact '66 had on me would be felt strongly through both the images and the text.

Whether you graduated high school in 1966, or started Little League, Campfire Girls, or Girl Scouts, or didn't find out about the '60s until the first Austin Powers movie in 1997, I hope this book will entertain you, and help you realize how many of the wonders of the era, which are still appreciated today, originated in this one remarkable year.

I also hope that, in reading my book, you begin to reacquaint yourself with your own happiest memories from childhood—from whatever your favorite year might be.

Note: *In putting this book together, I have striven to use only the most accurate visual representations available—photos and artifacts that are actually from 1966. In a few rare instances in which images of '66 icons were not available, I used images from other years to represent them.*

ACKNOWLEDGMENTS
BY HAL LIFSON

I want to profoundly thank all those who helped make this tribute to my favorite year a literary reality:

Jeffrey Stern, you allowed me to fulfill a life's dream, and for that I am so grateful. Your leadership and long-term friendship were the foundations of this project. Catherine Lorenz, your brilliant and extraordinary artistic talent (and patience) made this book so special. Hey, my second book will be easier, I promise! Devon Freeny, your thorough editing and all-around creative work was outstanding and invaluable. I could never have done this book without your countless hours of dedicated effort and careful eye for detail. Brigitte Urbina, heartfelt thanks for all your help with editorial matters, and for your passionate devotion to my book, even when you had contracts to negotiate! I am eternally grateful; you are solid evidence that 1966 was indeed a special year. Keith Barrows, thanks for all your diligent efforts scanning and organizing my images. I hope you know how much I appreciate all your hard work. Cheers, mate! Mark London, for the many hours you spent locating, scanning, and fixing up images in Photoshop—and for your insight and unwavering dedication—thank you. Nancy Sinatra, thank you for your friendship and boundless generosity since 1994. You inspired me to see this project through. And, of course, thanks for all the beautiful photos. Brian and Melinda Wilson, thanks so much for adding "good vibes" to my music chapter. Adam West, thank you for being my first hero. David Cohen, thanks for being a great role model and neighbor. Fred Wostbrock, thanks for all your help with photos—and comic relief. Kevin Burns, thanks for all the terrific photos, and your support and encouragement over the years. Joe Russo, thanks for all the hours of long-distance calls discussing the '60s. Allison Milionis, thanks for the copy assistance and editorial input. Cindy Gold, thanks to you and your staff at JCH Studios for the excellent still photography. Neville Johnson, thanks for sharing your knowledge of and love for the '60s. Mark Sullivan, thanks for all the help with the scanning. Rodney Bingenheimer, thanks to "the mayor of the Sunset Strip" for your inspiration, knowledge, and enthusiasm about the music of all decades.

And, finally, thanks to my family—Mom, Dad, Bobby, and Byrdie—for all the happy years since 1966!

TV GUIDE

WHOSE TV TESTS • *page 6* • SPY GIMMICKS • *page 14* • VIRGINIA GRAHAM • *page 33*

15¢ • LOCAL PROGRAMS • APRIL 2-8

DEAN MARTIN

Channel ThirTEEN
KCOP TELEVISION, INC.
915 NORTH LA BREA • HOLLYWOOD
Entrance: Willoughby Street Side

LIVE!
6:00
MONDAY
THRU
FRIDAY
AFTERNOONS

DOORS CLOSE
AT
4:30 PM

Let's all TWIST to . . .
THAXTON'S SHOW
TEEN-tunes, Disc Stars & Dancing
starring LLOYD THAXTON

ADMIT ONE FREE

DELL
08-919-701

WHO'S WHO IN TELEVISION

HUNDREDS OF PHOTOS AND LIFE STORIES

No. 16 35¢

GIANT BONUS SECTION
Complete Casts and Ratings of First Run Hollywood Movies on TV this Year

VAUGHN & McCALLUM

U.N.C.L.E. GETS A NEW GIRL

THE LENNON SISTERS

GOING THEIR SEPARATE WAYS?

ALL THE NEW SHOWS AND STARS *plus* THE RETURNING ONES

NIGHTLY PROGRAM GUIDE FOR 1966-67

STANWYCK

FEUDING IN THE BIG VALLEY?

GREEN HORNET

STEALING BATMAN'S THUNDER?

TV GUIDE

IS TELEVISION UP TO ITS GREATEST CHALLENGE
By Eric F. Goldman
see page 7

LOCAL PROGRAMS • MARCH 26-APRIL 1
15¢

POW

ADAM WEST
AS BATMAN

1
TELEVISION

Television was without a doubt the most powerful and influential medium of the year 1966. I was in the first grade this year, and every day at school I would share stories with my friends about the shows that we had watched the night before. It was a supreme bonding experience. Of course, a big part of the bonding had to do with what TV characters were on your lunchbox—for me, it was the *Peanuts* gang.

In Los Angeles, as in many local markets around the country, many stations aired early-morning kids' shows with fabulous live hosts who would start each day off on just the right note. I remember watching the incredible *Hobo Kelly* on local Channel 11, which was KTTV. She would soon move to Channel 13, KCOP—their cool diamond-shaped logo always stuck in my mind.

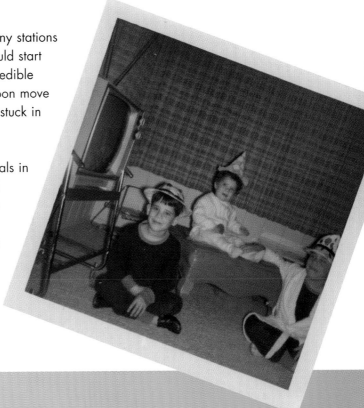

Hobo Kelly was played by Sally Baker. Along with her puppet pals in Hobo Junction, she would keep you entertained until the carpool showed up. This was the first children's show that used the "blue screen" technique, which allowed Hobo Kelly to enter other, magical worlds or talk to a huge giant right out of "Jack and the Beanstalk." This was a groundbreaking educational show that lasted for over ten years on Los Angeles television.

HOBO KELLY

WINNER OF THE GOLDEN RULE AWARD ACCLAIMED THE MOST CREATIVE AND IMAGINATIVE CHILDREN'S SHOW ON THE AIR.

KCOP 13

MONDAY thru FRIDAY
3:30 to 4:30 PM/COLOR

Another favorite kids' show—which had a significant adult following—was *Shrimpenstein*. This show featured a mini-Frankenstein puppet with loads of attitude! The humor was very satirical and the host of the show, Dr. Rudolph Von Schtick, had a rough time dealing with all the zany monster puppet characters in Von Schtick Castle.

Shrimpenstein ran on local Channel 9 in L.A., and fans like Frank Sinatra and Sammy Davis, Jr., tuned in at 5:00 P.M. every night to see the wild *MAD* magazine–type humor. The show was done live and was the first program to showcase the *Marvel Superhero* cartoons of '66.

These cartoons are most memorable for their ridiculously stilted animation—actual comic panels were photographed, and shaken back and forth to give the appearance of movement. The cartoon series was very dramatic and featured five of the most well-known Marvel Comics characters: Iron Man, the Sub-Mariner, Captain America, the Incredible Hulk, and the Mighty Thor.

I was not overly familiar with these characters from comic books as I generally read DC Comics, which were more accessible, with friendly superheroes who smiled—like Batman, Superman, and the Teen Titans. The Marvel characters were much more brooding and cerebral.

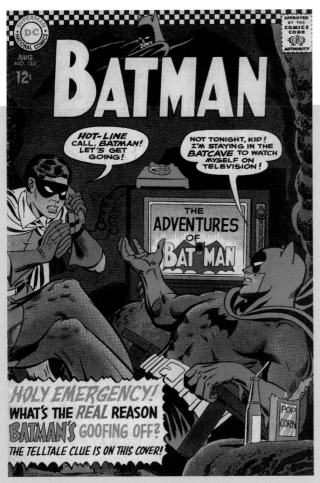

Television in 1966 was dominated by the superhero trend, which was launched on January 12 with the debut of *Batman* on ABC. It was unlike any show before it—a hip blend of pop art, comic books, satire, camp, and adventure.

Adam West and Burt Ward (whose real name was Burton "Sparky" Gervis) played the Caped Crusaders to absolute perfection. Along with millions of other kids around the country, I was mesmerized as I watched Batman and Robin foil the Riddler, the Penguin, the Joker, and Mr. Freeze, all within the first five weeks of broadcast!

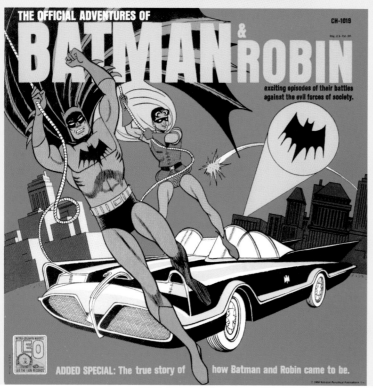

THE OFFICIAL ADVENTURES OF

BATMAN & ROBIN

CH-1019

exciting episodes of their battles against the evil forces of society.

ADDED SPECIAL: The true story of how Batman and Robin came to be.

CHARTER MEMBER
Batman & Robin Society

Batman was the first show I knew of to air two consecutive nights per week. It was a pop culture phenomenon that inspired a *huge* merchandising craze. I treasured my Batman collectibles, and watching this incredible program provided me with the most memorable hours of television I experienced during the '60s.

Batman had a unique style of television filming that concentrated on bright colors, incredible costumes, imaginative set design, and marvelous performances by guest villains.

Of course, the standout for me was Julie Newmar's Catwoman—she probably taught me more about the allure of femininity than my Betty and Veronica comics did. Julie Newmar was definitely my first television sex symbol. Every time I heard "What's New Pussycat?" by Tom Jones (1965), I thought of her.

With her skin-tight black jumpsuit and matching go-go boots, Julie looked like her body had been dipped in molten licorice. She was a ballet dancer, and she had the *femme fatale* bit down to a science. It was such fun watching her try to seduce Batman, even though as a six-year-old kid I respected him for resisting her. She had starred in a TV series earlier in the '60s (*My Living Doll* with Bob Cummings on CBS, on which she played Rhoda the Robot), and had given a Tony Award–winning Broadway performance in *The Marriage-Go-Round*, but it was her work on *Batman* that really brought her acclaim. In the *Batman* movie of '66, Julie was unavailable to play the role of Catwoman, so Lee Meriwether stepped in and really made the role work, in a different way than Julie, but sexy just the same.

In the fall of 1966, Lee Meriwether appeared as a guest star on *Family Affair* as the girlfriend of Uncle Bill (Brian Keith). Lee was one of the stars of *The Time Tunnel* in '66 as Dr. Ann MacGregor. Lee's co-stars on *The Time Tunnel* were James Darren and Robert Colbert. Each week, they would land in a different period of history, tumbling onto the scene in their cool turtlenecks—they never had to wear jackets, even when they were on board the Titanic or in Sherwood Forest! The series, which lasted only one year, was producer/creator Irwin Allen's third TV series of the '60s. *Voyage to the Bottom of the Sea* and *Lost in Space* were the first two.

Lost in Space was in its second season in 1966 and it was the first time the show was seen in color. I didn't really watch the show too much then, as it was on opposite *Batman*. The costumes of the Space Family Robinson were pretty colorful and Jetsons-like, and I remember liking that aspect of the program. Billy Mumy, who played young Will Robinson, always reminded me of Alfred E. Neuman. The Robot seemed like too much of a fuddy-duddy, though, and Dr. Smith disturbed me with his incessant whining.

Batman ignited an explosive trend of superhero shows and themes on TV. In the fall of '66, CBS dubbed its entire Saturday-morning lineup "Super Saturday." Super Saturday featured standout cartoons like Hanna-Barbera's *Frankenstein, Jr.*, based on the Japanese cartoon *Gigantor*, which had premiered on American TV in early '66. Also featured on *Frankenstein, Jr.* were the Impossibles, a rock group that doubled as superheroes. Another CBS cartoon was *Space Ghost*, which starred an intergalactic warrior voiced by Gary Owens.

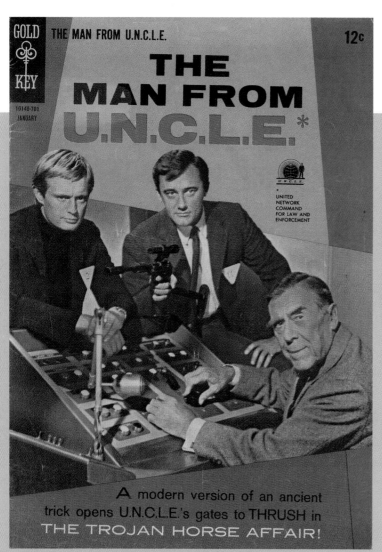

The bat craze affected shows in prime time as well. *The Man from U.N.C.L.E.*, then in its third season, switched away from traditional espionage plotlines to more over-the-top, even campy storylines. A spin-off show, *The Girl from U.N.C.L.E.*, starring Stefanie Powers as April Dancer (ably assisted by Noel Harrison as Mark Slate) premiered in the fall.

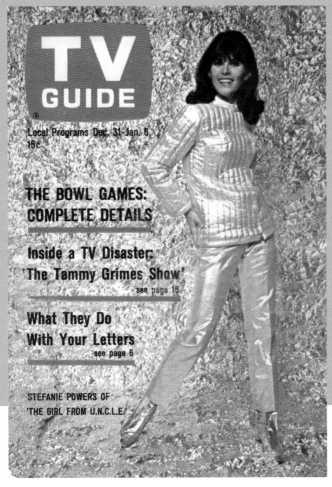

The Girl from U.N.C.L.E. was actually television's second super-spy chick. *Honey West* starring Anne Francis had debuted in the fall of '65 and was still in its network run from January through May of '66. Honey West first appeared on an episode of *Burke's Law*, and then was spun off onto her own show with a very cool array of high-tech (for 1966) gadgets. Lipstick walkie-talkies, exploding smoke bomb earrings, and a kicky convertible sports car (with car phone) were *de rigueur*. Her leading man and partner, Sam Bolt, was always helping her out of scrapes, although Honey West knew judo and took on the guys pretty well all by herself. *The Girl from U.N.C.L.E.* was more of a Carnaby Street–clad sleuth, who was not as physically confrontational as Honey West, but was also alluring.

Both *Honey West* and *The Girl from U.N.C.L.E.* disappeared after one season, but they were memorable for the liberated, "tough chick" personas of the female leads. Although both of them had male partners, they were independent women who were ahead of their time.

A couple other phenomenal shows of 1966 were: *T.H.E. Cat*, a show about a former circus aerialist/cat burglar who worked as a bodyguard for hire. Very film noir. It starred Robert Loggia as T. Hewitt Edward Cat. This character was based on both James Bond and Cary Grant's character in *To Catch a Thief*. Bond's enduring appeal also fueled interest in the British TV series *Danger Man*, starring Patrick McGoohan as international super-spy John Drake. The series was renamed *Secret Agent* when syndicated in the U.S., and the American broadcasts also changed the theme song to Johnny Rivers's famous "Secret Agent Man." Great dramatic show.

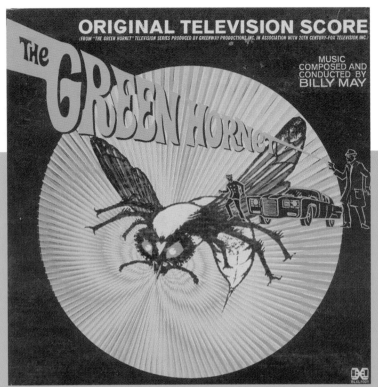

Also to emerge from the superhero craze was perhaps the coolest show of 1966: *The Green Hornet*, which starred Van Williams as the masked vigilante and Bruce Lee (making his debut) as Kato, the martial arts expert who assisted him in crime-bashing. The show was produced by the same team as *Batman* (executive producer William Dozier and Greenway Productions) but was done as a serious crime drama with great gadgetry and visuals.

The character had originated in a 1940s radio drama, but the Green Hornet of the '60s was more of a metropolitan James Bond. Britt Reid, owner and publisher of the *Daily Sentinel*, was a playboy by day, a masked crime avenger by night.

The Green Hornet was not as popular with kids as *Batman*. Although it was a very hip cult show, it only lasted for one season. Nevertheless, there were a lot of great *Green Hornet* merchandising tie-ins and, to this day, it is one of my favorite TV shows of all time. One big reason was the Green Hornet's secretary, Miss Lenore Case, played by the stunning Wende Wagner.

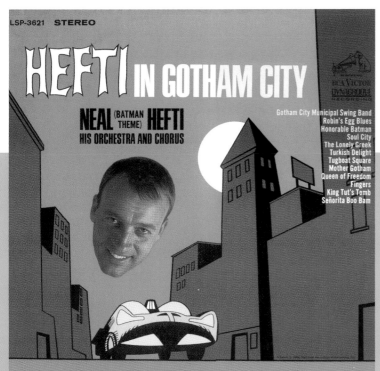

LSP-3621 STEREO

HEFTI IN GOTHAM CITY

NEAL (BATMAN THEME) HEFTI
HIS ORCHESTRA AND CHORUS

RCA VICTOR
DYNAGROOVE
RECORDING

Gotham City Municipal Swing Band
Robin's Egg Blues
Honorable Batman
Soul City
The Lonely Greek
Turkish Delight
Tugboat Square
Mother Gotham
Queen of Freedom
Fingers
King Tut's Tomb
Señorita Boo Bam

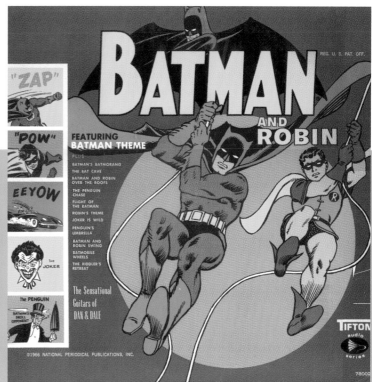

"ZAP"
"POW"
EEYOW
The JOKER
The PENGUIN
BATMAN'S DROLL OPPONENT

BATMAN
AND ROBIN

REG. U. S. PAT. OFF.

FEATURING
BATMAN THEME

PLUS

BATMAN'S BATMORANG
THE BAT CAVE
BATMAN AND ROBIN
OVER THE ROOFS
THE PENGUIN CHASE
FLIGHT OF THE BATMAN
ROBIN'S THEME
JOKER IS WILD
PENGUIN'S UMBRELLA
BATMAN AND ROBIN SWING
BATMOBILE WHEELS
THE RIDDLER'S RETREAT

The Sensational Guitars of DAN & DALE

TIFTON
audio series

©1966 NATIONAL PERIODICAL PUBLICATIONS, INC.

78002

Both *The Green Hornet* and *Batman* had memorable soundtrack tie-in albums and spin-off music albums that were really unique and fun to listen to while wearing my mock Hornet attire. (I used a green Halloween mask and my yellow vinyl raincoat to emulate the outfit.) My favorite was this obscure album by the Bat Boys, which had great instrumental organ music on it that reminded me of Booker T. and the MGs. Al Hirt, the Dixie trumpet man, did the *Green Hornet* TV theme. The *Green Hornet* soundtrack album on vinyl now sells for about three hundred dollars—if you can find one.

STEREO STEREO STEREO STEREO STEREO STEREO STEREO STER

DESIGN records

BATMAN

THEME

! AS ON THE ABC TV. TELEVISION SERIES BATMAN!

&

POW! WHAM! HOLY SMOKE! BLAM!
THE BATMAN THEME! MIGHTY MAYHEM! CHEATIN' CHARLIE! UPPERCUT BLUES! FIGHT FLIGHT!!!
AAARGH! BAP! UGH! ZOWIE!
THE VILLAIN STRIKES! OUT WITH THE IN CROWD! BEHIND THE 8 BALL! MARS VISITOR! ITS MURDER!
FEATURING THE SENSATIONAL BATBOYS!

Babara Eden starred in her first all-color season of *I Dream of Jeannie* this year on NBC. Four years later, she married Major Nelson (Larry Hagman) in the final season.

1966 was the debut year for TV's most famous producer-created rock group: *The Monkees*. They already had a smash record when the show premiered on NBC—"Last Train To Clarksville." The show was based on the wild visual style of the Beatles films *A Hard Day's Night* and *Help!*

Star Trek first aired in 1966—and went on to become a worldwide phenomenon. It is probably the most successful TV series of all time in terms of the popular spin-offs it spawned. I was never that into the show as a kid, but I grew to really appreciate its philosophical morality plays more as I got older in the '70s.

Gillligan's Island began its final season on CBS in the fall of '66. Only the second- and third-season shows would be used in later rebroadcasts; the first-season black-and-white shows were not seen as much until the Turner Broadcasting Company colorized them in the late '80s.

It's About Time, from *Gilligan's Island* producer Sherwood Schwartz, starred Joe Ross and Imogene Coca as part of a family of cave-dwellers who encounter two astronauts from modern times who are forced to cope with Neanderthal life. The far-fetched premise did not click with viewers like *Gilligan*, so the show was a one-season wonder. Ironically, two years later a similar premise became the basis for the hit film *Planet of the Apes*.

GOLD KEY
10195-701

IT'S ABOUT TIME   12c

It's About Time

It's a merry orbit-go-round!
Two astronauts break
the time barrier and land
back in the Stone Age!

© 1966 BY REDWOOD-CLADASYA-UATV

THE GRINCH
IN REPOSE

TOMORROW NIGHT * HOLIDAY SPECIAL * TOMORROW NIGHT

DR. SEUSS'
HOW The
GRINCH STOLE
CHRISTMAS

The fabled
story world of
DR. SEUSS
comes to television
for the first time
in this colorful
special for the
whole family!

narrated by
BORIS KARLOFF

7:00 P. M. CHANNEL 2

TOMORROW NIGHT * HOLIDAY SPECIAL * TOMORROW NIGHT

Two major animated holiday specials that debuted in 1966: *How the Grinch Stole Christmas* and *It's the Great Pumpkin, Charlie Brown*

Jay Ward, who produced the Rocky and Bullwinkle cartoons and, in 1967, *George of the Jungle*, also produced my favorite cartoon of 1966, *Hoppity Hooper*. Hoppity, Uncle Waldo, and Fillmore the bear were reminiscent of characters in *The Wind in the Willows* by Kenneth Grahame. *Hoppity Hooper* was unique in that it was cleverly written but still wacky. One show was a spoof of *The Twilight Zone* in which Hoppity and his pals were turned into vegetables in the "Traffic Zone."

After the cancellation of the witty, often ribald series *The Addams Family* (ABC), the two principal stars, John Astin and Carolyn Jones, both guested on *Batman*. Astin was the second actor to play the Riddler, but he could not compare with Riddler number one, Frank Gorshin. Carolyn played "Marsha, Queen of Diamonds" and actually got to marry Batman! Holy alimony!

Also on its final fins was *Flipper*, a charming show that began its last season in the fall of 1966. I loved the theme song and the animated opening titles. The underwater photography was handled by expert producer Ivan Tors, who also supervised the ambitious deep-sea footage of this year's Bond film, *Thunderball*. Flipper had an unflappable, near-human personality, and he inspired me to become a big fan of the Miami Dolphins football team. My buddies and I did Flipper impressions in the pool.

While many of my friends had strict parental restrictions on their TV viewing hours, my folks were pretty liberal about letting my brother and me watch our favorite shows after school and in the early evening. The hours I spent watching TV in 1966 broadened my horizons beyond Ventura Boulevard.

Local channels and the three major networks presented shows that had all the variety and cleverness I loved about the '60s as a decade. Throughout the years, I have watched and re-watched many of these brilliant TV shows, and I still feel the same passion about them to this day. Only now I don't pin the bath towel to my shoulders with safety pins when I watch *Batman* reruns.

Premiering this year (October 17) was *The Hollywood Squares*, one of television's longest-running and most appealing game shows. Host Peter Marshall would stay with the show until 1981; he played perfectly against regular guest stars like Rose Marie, Wally "Underdog" Cox, and Paul Lynde, who would make the center square his permanent home in 1968. Another legendary game show premiere: *The Newlywed Game* with host Bob Eubanks, which first aired on July 11.

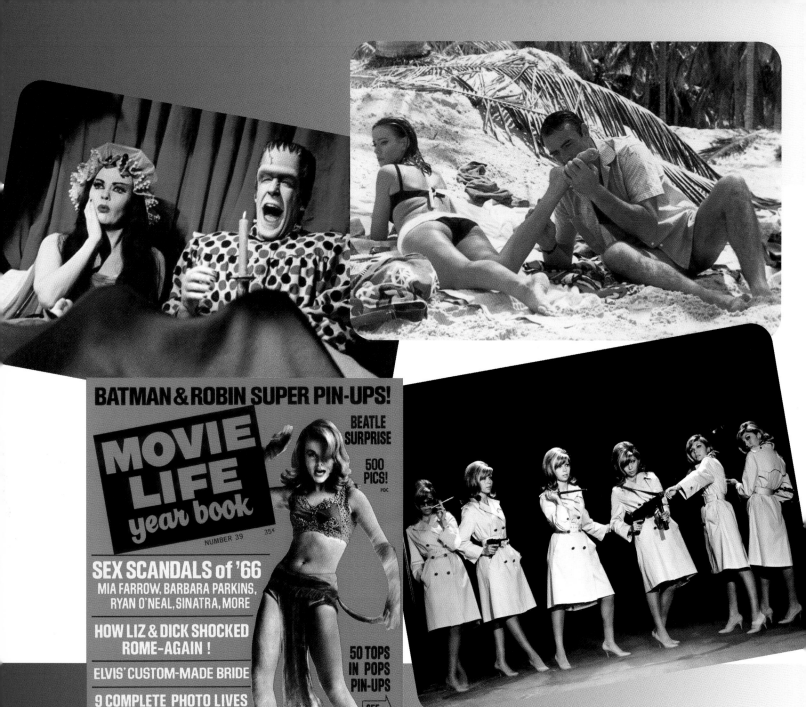

BATMAN & ROBIN SUPER PIN-UPS!

BEATLE SURPRISE

MOVIE LIFE year book

500 PICS!
PDC

NUMBER 39   35¢

SEX SCANDALS of '66
MIA FARROW, BARBARA PARKINS,
RYAN O'NEAL, SINATRA, MORE

HOW LIZ & DICK SHOCKED
ROME—AGAIN !

ELVIS' CUSTOM-MADE BRIDE

9 COMPLETE PHOTO LIVES

McCALLUM'S BARBED WIRE WALL

WIN JIM (BYRDS) McGUINN'S
SPECS

50 TOPS
IN POPS
PIN-UPS

SEE
BACK
COVER

ANN-MARGRET

Ideal
MAGAZINE

2 CINEMA

There can be no doubt—1966 was one of the most eclectic and prolific years in offbeat filmmaking.

I have generally been of the opinion that, during the '60s, movies were largely aimed at adults, while television was aimed primarily at kids and their parents. I remember watching films on television that year that had made their theatrical debuts in previous decades. It was on television that I first saw the first two Beatles films, *A Hard Day's Night* and *Help!*, as well as the classic Universal horror films of the '30s and '40s. I watched silent films with Charlie Chaplin, and movies with W.C. Fields and Buster Keaton. This was also the time during which I first encountered Laurel and Hardy and the Three Stooges, both in their original films and in the animated series based on them.

On the other hand, several of the most memorable film releases of 1966 were based on TV series—which made them a spectacular thrill for me to see on the big screen. When I was a kid, my mom would drop my friends and me off at the Encino Theater. I remember the unique '50s astrospace design of the marquee and how exciting it was to be there for a Saturday matinee. I also remember going with my parents to the Sepulveda or Van Nuys Drive-Ins, where many of my most precious cinematic memories were created in this very special year. My brother, Bob, was usually asleep in the back of my mom's station wagon halfway through the first feature. That was okay with me, as I would inherit his Junior Mints and rapidly melting Bon Bons.

1.
BATMAN

This was the spectacular feature film based on the ABC TV show, which had just concluded its first smash season in prime-time. Zowie! All four supervillains—the Riddler, the Joker, the Penguin, and the Catwoman—in one phenomenal Batman adventure . . . could life get much better?

Julie Newmar had made one appearance on the TV series as Catwoman, but she was unavailable for the feature film, so Lee Meriwether stepped into the catsuit and played the role brilliantly. To me, this is Lee Meriwether's signature performance, in which she plays both Catwoman and her alter ego Miss Kitka, the Russian journalist from the *Moscow Bugle*. It is the cunningly seductive Miss Kitka who almost manages to purloin Bruce Wayne's affections during their unforgettable "night on the town" in Gotham City.

The Batman movie is a true classic and was a special thrill for millions of Batfans in the summer of '66. The DVD version was released recently and it's still hilarious, not only for Batman's battle with a foam rubber shark, but also for the audio commentary performed by stars Burt Ward and Adam West.

20th Century-Fox presents "BATMAN" starring ADAM WEST · BURT WARD
Guest Villains: Lee Meriwether as "The Catwoman" · Cesar Romero as "The Joker"
Burgess Meredith as "The Penguin" · Frank Gorshen as "The Riddler"
Produced by William Dozier · Directed by Leslie H. Martinson · Screenplay by Lorenzo Semple, Jr.
Color by De Luxe · A 20th Century-Fox—Greenlawn Productions, Inc.

2.
THUNDERBALL

Actually released in late '65, but it played in theaters into the spring of '66.

This fourth installment of the James Bond franchise was indeed the "Biggest Bond of Them All," with spectacular underwater photography and fight sequences. This film reminded me of a big-budget version of my favorite early '60s TV series, *Sea Hunt*, which starred Lloyd Bridges as scuba-diving detective Mike Nelson. (*Sea Hunt* was one of several black-and-white TV series from producer Frederick Ziv, the other three being *Highway Patrol*, *Ripcord*, and *Whirlybirds*.)

Thunderball was a phenomenon that generated the Bond films' biggest box-office receipts of the decade. The previous Bond film, *Goldfinger* (1964) had also been huge, and was the first Bond adventure to feature a "supervillain"—Auric Goldfinger, played by Gert Frobe. *Thunderball* followed suit, featuring Adolfo Celi as the suave but power-mad Emilio Largo.

Sean Connery returned as the gallant secret agent. This time he romanced the exquisite former Miss France, Claudine Auger, who beat out even Raquel Welch for the role of Domino, Largo's ambivalent mistress. Bond made a big impression on the delectable Domino by biting her foot on the beach in order to remove poisonous sea egg spines. "I've never tasted women before. They're quite good," Bond exclaims, like the ultimate macho mensch he always is.

Thunderball also featured a bevy of bodacious beauties—Luciana Paluzzi as *femme fatale* Fiona Volpe; Martine Beswick as Paula, Bond's assistant in the Bahamas; and Molly Peters as Patricia Fearing, the

buxom health spa masseuse with whom Bond hits the showers. After a hedonistic session with Patricia and the notorious "mink glove," Bond abruptly leaves the room. "Where are you going?" she asks. "I thought I would take a little exercise," Connery replies. "You must be joking!" Patricia says, wrapping herself in a blue bedsheet.

Even at age six, I was highly appreciative of these Aqua Velva moments, and Sean Connery has remained my greatest hero to this day. I remember it was in 1966 that I saw 007 cologne and hoped for a bottle to be tucked into my Christmas stocking. I was so disappointed when I found a new toothbrush instead!

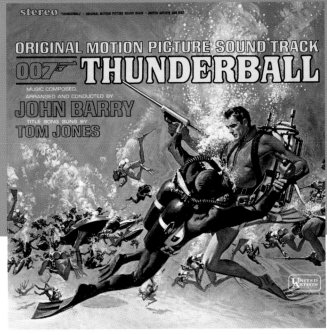

3.
THE SWINGER

Starring Ann-Margret: Wild, kicky sex comedy for the swingin' '60s set!

This is one of those heavily visual movies of the 1960s in which the story takes a backseat to the eye candy of the set design—and, in this case, of the lead actress. Completing director George Sidney's "trilogy" of cinematic love letters to Ann-Margret (the other two being *Viva Las Vegas* and *Bye Bye Birdie*), the story revolves around Kelly Olsson (Ann's character, who shares the actress' real last name), an aspiring short story author who poses as a bad girl to impress Tony Franciosa, the editor in chief of *Girl Lure* (read *Playboy*) magazine.

The highlight of the film is the scene in which Ann-Margret swirls around in colored paints like a human Handi-Wipe. This scene was featured in an October '66 *Playboy* pictorial which made my little watercolor paintbox seem that much more enticing.

The Swinger is now quite a rare film, and, to date, has never been released on video and is rarely shown on TV. It includes many scenes of Los Angles circa 1966, most notably Ann-Margret's Laurel Canyon communal hideaway, where she performs a really scorching dance routine, lending new relevance to the black leotard. Another cool musical highlight is "I Wanna Be Loved," sung to tuxedoed Tony Franciosa, who looks either smitten or bemused because Ann's hair is blowing mysteriously, without an open window in the bedroom.

In *The Swinger*, as in many of her films, Ann-Margret exuded an intoxicating blend of schoolgirl innocence and "kitten with a whip" saucy sexuality that was unique and astonishing.

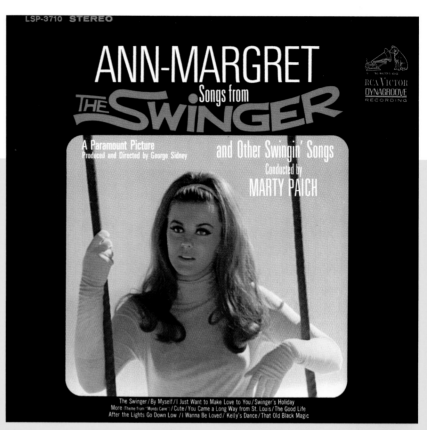

IT SWINGS LIKE NOTHING EVER SWUNG!

PARAMOUNT PICTURES PRESENTS

ANN-MARGRET and TONY FRANCIOSA in

The SWINGER

TECHNICOLOR®

A GEORGE SIDNEY PRODUCTION

CO-STARRING ROBERT COOTE · YVONNE ROMAIN · HORACE McMAHON

WRITTEN BY LAWRENCE ROMAN · DIRECTED AND PRODUCED BY GEORGE SIDNEY · TITLE SONG BY DORY AND ANDRE PREVIN

A PARAMOUNT PICTURE

4.
MUNSTER, GO HOME

Another sentimental favorite. The Munster family's last romp of the '60s, this time in Technicolor.

The Munster family debuted on the big screen just as their two-year stint on CBS was winding down. When the cast made this movie in 1966 they did not realize they would not be back for a third season in the fall. But, alas, the classic monster craze of the early '60s had begun to fade, overshadowed by *Batman* and the burgeoning superhero trend.

This was an extremely fun movie aimed at kids as a Saturday matinee feature. Fred Gwynne and Al Lewis made appearances around the country, along with the Munster coach, to promote the film for Universal Pictures. Also featured in this movie was Grandpa's souped-up "Drag-u-la." It was created by George Barris, who also designed the Munster Koach. I still enjoy watching this film today (it was recently released on DVD), as I am immediately transported back to the Reseda walk-in theater in the Valley, where I watched this film while eating Flicks candies by Ghirardelli, which were chocolate wafers that came in a little cardboard tube with colored foil wrapping.

Munster, Go Home is very Disney-like in its feel and visual approach, and it captures the warmth and humor of the TV series perfectly. In the film, Herman and his family travel to jolly ol' England to claim a castle they have inherited. Debbie Watson, a teen actress who had starred in the TV series *Tammy* before making this movie, became the third Marilyn (following Beverley Owen and Pat Priest) and brought a Gidget-like flair to the role. The next year, Watson starred with Roddy McDowall in a movie send-up of teen culture called *The Cool Ones*.

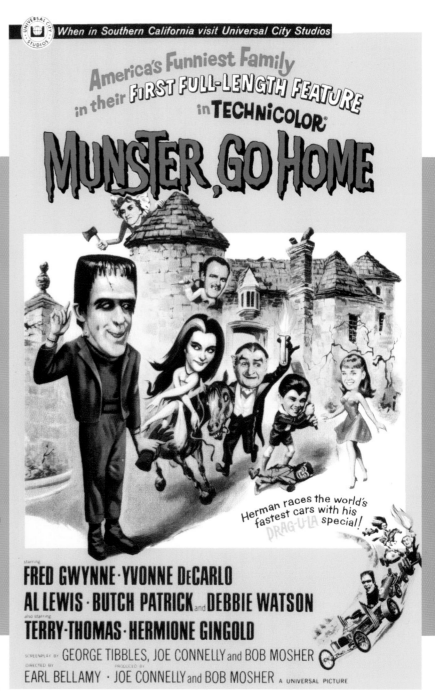

Munster, Go Home was one of a series of youth-oriented films that Universal Pictures delivered in 1966. Another notable title was the spy spoof *Out of Sight*. Distinctive visuals, a hip-shakin' go-go dance sequence by Deanna Lund as "Tuff Bod," and a kool dragster called the ZZR (designed by George Barris) make this a cult favorite. Also out from Universal Pictures this year was the film *Wild, Wild Winter*, one of the lost classics of the teen film genre. It featured a rare on-screen musical performance by the Beau Brummels, who the year before had big hits with "Laugh, Laugh" and "Just a Little." They had also made a memorable cameo on *The Flintstones* as the Beau Brummelstones.

5.
WHAT'S UP, TIGER LILY?

One of Woody Allen's funniest, most off-the-wall comedies, although not a box-office smash.

Woody took a Japanese spy film from 1964 called *Kagi No Kag* or "Key of Keys" (which in itself was a campy send-up of the Bond genre), and dubbed the original characters' voices with American actors. The new dialogue tells a different story entirely—one that loosely revolves around the stealing of the world's best egg salad recipe. The movie was one of many James Bond parodies to hit the big screen in 1966.

The film featured several songs by the popular rock group the Lovin' Spoonful, whose notable hits this year were "Daydream," "Summer in the City," and "Did You Ever Have to Make Up Your Mind."

Woody had just come off the success of 1965's *What's New, Pussycat?*, which was his first screenwriting credit. Although he was reportedly unhappy with how that film eventually turned out, it was popular with audiences. The title *What's Up, Tiger Lily?* was a spoof on his previous film's title.

At the end of *What's Up, Tiger Lily?* is a very memorable cameo striptease by *Playboy* Playmate China Lee, one of the most popular centerfolds of the decade. She appeared in many '60s movies like *The Swinger* and *Dr. Goldfoot and the Bikini Machine*. She also appeared on TV shows, including a very cool episode of *The Man from U.N.C.L.E.* entitled "The Discotheque Affair."

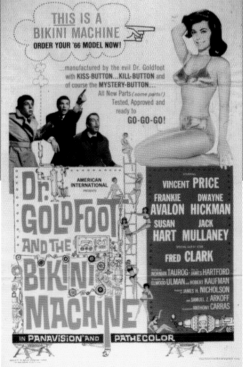

James Coburn made the first of two appearances as the karate-crunching man about world, American super-spy Derek Flint. These films were major influences on *Austin Powers* (1997) and its sequels. The artist who designed *Our Man Flint*'s movie poster and soundtrack album cover was Bob Peak, whose bold and unique sense of design was evident in the many '60s movie posters he created. His choice of images for this project really captures the film's opulent vision of a male fantasy world of martial arts, handguns, and scantily clad women.

Also debuting in 1966 was Dean Martin as super-agent Matt Helm in the first of four feature-film appearances. *The Silencers*, with its memorable opening dance sequence by Cyd Charisse, was a true spectacle. Dean Martin was the height of cool this year, seen here with co-star Dahlia Lavi. The Matt Helm films were also obvious inspiration for Austin Powers and were notable for their colorful and creative set design. Sequels were *Murderers' Row* (1966), *The Ambushers* (1967), and *The Wrecking Crew* (1969).

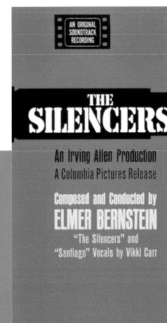

THE SILENCERS

An Irving Allen Production
A Columbia Pictures Release

Composed and Conducted by
ELMER BERNSTEIN
"The Silencers" and
"Santiago" Vocals by Vikki Carr

Matt Helm,
Secret Agent,
assigned to the
deadliest missions
with the liveliest
companions

OC-1120

The Man Called Flintstone, the second animated Hanna-Barbera feature film (the first was 1964's *Hey There, It's Yogi Bear*), created an alter ego for Fred Flintstone in the guise of super-agent Rock Slag, to capitalize on the mega-success of *Thunderball*.

This film was produced quickly, and did not have the pacing of the TV series, but it was still a treat to see the Flintstones on the big screen. Like *Munster, Go Home*, this film was done just as the series was ending its six-year prime-time run on ABC. Of course, many more adventures of *The Flintstones* would follow on Saturday mornings for several decades. Their next feature-length film would not come out until the '80s, when *The Jetsons Meet the Flintstones* was produced as an animated TV movie.

Modesty Blaise, a cool spy chick who in 1966 was the lead character in a production starring Italian beauty Monica Vitti. This film was very cartoon-like, but very adult, so I didn't come to know it until much later (the '80s). It was kind of a precursor to *Barbarella* (1968) in the way that it brought the pop-art medium to the big screen.

Modesty Blaise was a popular European comic book character, like Barbarella, and both were clearly not intended for the youth market

Casino Royale, the cult-classic send-up of the Bond world, began filming toward the end of 1966. This film is undeniably a major Austin Powers influence. A classic scene is the one in which the stunningly beautiful Ursula Andress attempts to seduce debonair secret agent Evelyn Tremble . . . or is it the other way around? Dusty Springfield's gorgeous "The Look of Love" plays underneath this scene, and launches this film into the pop culture hall of fame.

Dr. Goldfoot and the Girl Bombs, the 1966 sequel to 1965's Dr. Goldfoot and the Bikini Machine. This one was filmed in Italy, and Vincent Price returned in the title role.

The Last of the Secret Agents? was a spy comedy starring Marty Allen and Steve Rossi, and Nancy Sinatra in one of her big film roles of the year.

A memorable sequence in the film is one in which her waitress outfit gets caught on a doorknob to reveal a sexy black Frederick's of Hollywood ensemble underneath.

A carbon copy of *Our Man Flint*, *The Liquidator* starred Australian actor Rod Taylor, who first came to prominence in Alfred Hitchcock's *The Birds* (1963).

Run for Your Wife was typical of the wild, sexy comedy spoofs of the mid-'60s. This one starred Juliette Prowse and Rhonda Fleming.

Not with My Wife, You Don't! This was another fine outing for beautiful Italian actress Virna Lisi, who also starred with Frank Sinatra this year in *Assault on a Queen*. The year before, Lisi had starred with Jack Lemmon in *How to Murder Your Wife*.

Boy, Did I Get a Wrong Number! was a hilarious movie starring Bob Hope, Elke Sommer, and the irascible Phyllis Diller, who during her breakthrough year of 1966 created lunacy as Hope's housekeeper. This film and 1967's *Eight on the Lam* were two of Bob Hope's funniest films to me and are so memorable because I saw them at the same time I was enjoying my Bob Hope comic books. Elke Sommer shines as the spoiled bubble-bath starlet with whom Hope becomes entangled. One of her best roles since 1964's *A Shot in the Dark*.

Spinout was the big Elvis film of '66. Here the King enjoys a poolside chick-fest. This film was one of many musical comedies Elvis rolled out in the '60s, and this time he is back in his racecar with co-stars Shelly Fabares and Diane McBain.

Elvis and Diane McBain about to take the "Nestea Plunge."

How to Steal a Million: Another madcap crime caper, with Audrey Hepburn and Peter O'Toole. Note the artwork in the style of designer Bob Peak—always thin, long legs featured. Hepburn plays the daughter of an art forger who mistakenly involves private eye O'Toole in a robbery. Cool and classy flick.

Kaleidoscope stars Warren Beatty and Susannah York in a swingin' '60s affair. Beatty plays an American playboy (natch) who breaks into a playing card factory and marks the cards so he can win at every casino in Europe. I always thought they should open a card casino on Sunset Blvd. here in L.A. called "Strip Poker."

In *Alfie*, Michael Caine gives his quintessential 1960s performance as the lonely but well-spoken-for London bachelor. This film and *Georgy Girl* (Lynn Redgrave's star-making performance) are two of my favorite endearingly poignant British films of 1966. *Alfie* has a beautiful, haunting theme song performed by Dionne Warwick: "What's it all about, Alfie?"

Loopy, quirky Don Knotts hits the big screen with *The Ghost and Mr. Chicken*, another comedy horror movie from Universal Pictures, which also released *Munster, Go Home* in 1966. Knotts plays a nervous-nellie reporter who discovers ghosts in a small-town murder mansion.

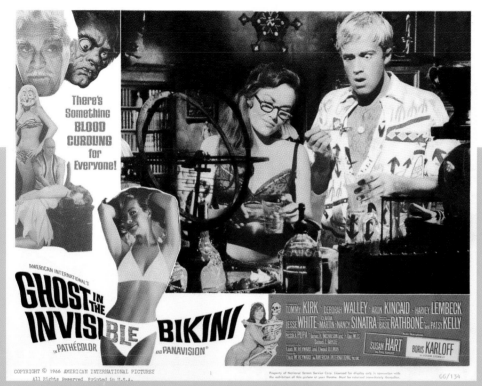

The Ghost in the Invisible Bikini: A wild beach-party romp in which a motorcycle gang gets involved with a Frankenstein's monster type at a haunted mansion. Boris Karloff makes one of his last film appearances here. A brunette Nancy Sinatra rocks out poolside with her little halter top in the rave-up "Geronimo," backed by the Bobby Fuller Four ("I Fought the Law"). This was American International's attempt to broaden the type of teen films they were producing, beyond just placing the kids at the beach. Other films like this would be *Ski Party*, *Sergeant Deadhead*, *Fireball 500*, and the Dr. Goldfoot films.

Soupy Sales, who had starred in his own TV show in the early '60s, makes a splash on the silver screen as a wacky janitor at an atomic power plant who is accidentally ionized and then can fly. I remember seeing this movie in a theater with one of my babysitters, Mrs. Lockwood. She drove a powder blue Plymouth station wagon that, to this day, sits in her driveway at her home in Encino, California. These offbeat children's comedies made up the bulk of my moviegoing experiences in 1966.

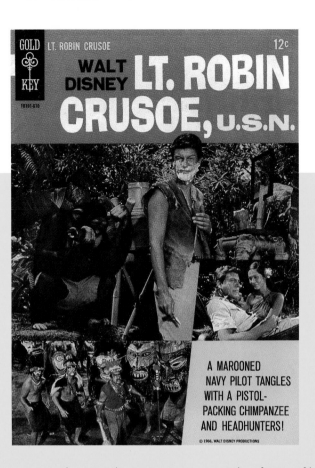

This was the Disney company's big feature film for 1966. *Lt. Robin Crusoe, U.S.N* starred Dick Van Dyke, who had starred two years earlier in *Mary Poppins* and was still starring in his own brilliant sitcom on CBS. This movie put him on a tropical isle with actress Nancy Kwan (who had starred with William Holden in 1960's *The World of Suzie Wong*) and a prankster chimpanzee. (Remember, monkeys were hot in '66 thanks to Micky Dolenz.) The screenplay for this film was based on a story by Retlaw Yesnid—which is "Walter Disney" spelled backward.

Other notable releses for the Disney studios in 1966: *The Ugly Dachsund*, starring Dean Jones and Suzanne Pleshette, and *Winnie the Pooh and the Honey Tree*. (This year, I remember, boxes of Wheat Honeys and Rice Honeys cereal contained plastic figures of the Pooh characters that fit on your spoon.)

Although obscure, *A Man and a Woman* is surely one of the best films to come out of Europe in 1966—it won Best Film at the Cannes Film Festival. I remember seeing this film on TV with subtitles and thinking, "What a masterpiece." Of course, this was many years after the '60s, when the tender but melancholy love story resonated with me as an adult with romantic entanglements of my own. Although mine usually revolved around my ATM card not working.

A Man and a Woman was also memorable for its beautiful theme song, composed by Francis Lai, and the Claudine Longet vocal version is one of the true classic records of its time. In this film, writer/director Claude Lelouch used expressionistic, avant garde techniques that quickly became the standard for TV advertising in Europe and the United States. Nineteen sixty-eight's *The Thomas Crown Affair* (directed by Norman Jewison) took its distinctive geometric camera angles from this film.

GRAND PRIX FESTIVAL INTERNATIONAL CANNES 1966

anouk aimée
jean-louis trintignant
pierre barouh
dans
un film de
claude lelouch

un homme
et une femme

avec la participation de
valérie lagrange
et simone paris

EASTMANCOLOR
une production les films 13
distribuée par les artistes associés

musique de francis lai saravah editions

The *Big TNT Show* was record producer extraordinaire Phil Spector's second filmed movie concert, after *The TAMI Show* in 1964. The all-star roster included Donovan, the Byrds, the Ronettes, and Bo Diddley, and Petula Clark performed an unforgettable version of "Downtown." Backing up these artists was Spector's famous group of studio musicians known as the "Wrecking Crew." Drummer Hal Blaine, keyboardist Don Randi, guitarist Tommy Tedesco, and bass player Carol Kaye made up the core rhythm section of this outstanding ensemble.

Grand Prix: James Garner, Jessica Walter, Eva Marie Saint, and Geneviève Page starred in this cult film about racecar drivers at Monte Carlo. This film is best remembered for its high-speed racing footage. To me, it was the adult version of the Japanese cartoon *Speed Racer*, which first appeared on American TV in 1966. The racing motif in children's cartoons continued in 1967 with "Tom Slick" (part of the *George of the Jungle* show), and in 1968 with *The Wacky Races*. Who wasn't a fan of Penelope Pitstop with her little pink a go-go sports car?

A FANTASTIC AND SPECTACULAR VOYAGE...
THROUGH THE HUMAN BODY...INTO THE BRAIN.

fantastic voyage

STARRING
Stephen Boyd, Raquel Welch, Edmond O'Brien, Donald Pleasence, Arthur O'Connell, William Redfield and Arthur Kennedy, Produced by Saul David, Directed by Richard Fleischer, Screenplay by Harry Kleiner, Adaptation by David Duncan, Music by Leonard Rosenman, CinemaScope, Color by DeLuxe.

20. CENTURY-FOX

Fantastic Voyage was Raquel Welch's big breakthrough film, which was paired with *One Million Years B.C.* C'mon . . . what cool kid didn't have the poster of stunning Raquel in the animal-skin bikini that year? *Fantastic Voyage* was the film that took Raquel out of the running for *Thunderball*, and it was in 1966 that she became the preeminent female sex symbol in pop culture, appearing on numerous magazine covers.

Amazingly, she has held onto this stature quite admirably for over thirty-five years. Raquel had tested for 1966's *Our Man Flint*, and in '67 she turned down a part in *Valley of the Dolls*. In December of 1979, Raquel appeared on the cover of *Playboy*. She has made a big comeback in recent years in film (*Legally Blonde*) and television.

Faster, Pussycat! Kill! Kill!: This was a hard-hitting, sadistic road movie from cult film director Russ Meyer, known for its gratuitous violence and sociopathic go-go vixens. They drive fast and break the necks of guys who take advantage of them. Not a film I saw as a kid, but when I did see it at an art house revival theater, I realized that it was a very well crafted black comedy. It is engrossing, if hard to watch, and it makes a powerful cinematic statement about women reacting to misogyny and chauvinism. Women's lib, meet the Hell's Angels.

Real-life Hell's Angels participated in the making of the road movie *The Wild Angels*, another tough one to watch. Nancy Sinatra starred with Peter Fonda and Bruce Dern, cementing her image as a biker rock chick.

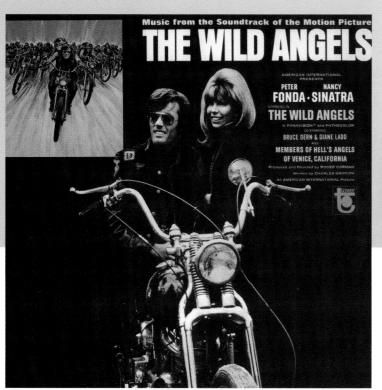

Lord Love a Duck is a dark comedy from writer/director George Axelrod. I discovered this film first through its very cool soundtrack by Neal Hefti, featuring an obscure group, the Wild Ones. Roddy McDowall gives a tour de force performance as the Svengali who hypnotizes beautiful Tuesday Weld and gives her everything she wants, but never seems to make her happy. It is sharp satire on current (for 1966) American culture and the generation gap. A highly underrated, funny film with a great cast that includes Harvey Korman and Ruth Gordon.

ORIGINAL MOTION PICTURE SOUND TRACK
music by NEAL HEFTI

GEORGE AXELROD'S

LORD LOVE A DUCK

AN ACT OF PURE AGGRESSION

WORLD-PACIFIC STEREO

THE ORIGINAL SOUND-TRACK MUSIC FROM

BRUCE BROWN'S

The Endless Summer

THE SANDALS

The Endless Summer is the definitive surfing film of the year 1966, and maybe of all time. It was completely conceived and photographed by filmmaker Bruce Brown, and he presented it as a documentary of both surfing and California culture as seen around the world.

My beach memories of 1966 take me back to Sorrento beach in Santa Monica. My family used to go to the Sorrento Grill and get cheeseburgers wrapped in yellow wax paper. Sometimes, my brother and I would play *The Time Tunnel* and tumble onto the sand as if we had arrived in a prehistoric world. It was hard to maintain this façade while seeing my mom read her *Valley of the Dolls* paperback and eat barbecue chips. Listening to my transistor radio at the beach, tuned into 93 KHJ, I would hear "Summer in the City" and think it was about Los Angeles.

Just as summer was a relief from the pressures of grade school, movies were a way of escaping to faraway places and imaginary lands. Although my family didn't travel much this year, each film I saw was a vacation all its own. Whereas television offered light entertainment in the safety of my own home, the larger-than-life visual grandeur of the movies was all-encompassing and, at times, overwhelming.

These films made me more aware of just how small I still was. . . .

3 SOUNDS

No year in my life has been better for music than 1966. This incredible year encapsulated everything that was groundbreaking and timeless about the music of the '60s.

As a kid in '66, I listened to an amazingly diverse collection of sounds on my pocket transistor radio. I found the music so exciting that I would keep my transistor turned on underneath my pillow at night so I could go to sleep serenaded by groups like the Byrds, Sonny and Cher, the Turtles, and even Herb Alpert and the Tijuana Brass. Sometimes I would pull my parents' wicker rocking chair into my room and rock for hours while listening to the radio and my records. One of the things that made my childhood so memorable was monitoring "teen culture" through hours and hours of listening to contests, deejay patter, and advertising on the radio.

I remember listening to ads for the Hollywood Teenage Fair, where many of the local L.A. rock groups performed. Pacific Ocean Park, the amusement park at Venice Beach, also hosted many rock groups, including Gary Lewis and the Playboys. During the summer of '66, I would daydream of attending places like this, eating cotton candy and caramel apples while surrounded by teenagers in colorful summer attire. I also recall hearing exciting announcements for big concerts this year like the Beatles at Dodger Stadium, and shows at the Whisky A Go Go and Valley Music Center. The Valley Music Center was a space-age architectural wonder—a huge, white, dome-shaped building that had a theater-in-the-round setup and a rotating stage. It hosted many top-flight rock groups, including the Doors and the Byrds. It also served as a showcase for mainstream pop singers; I remember seeing Sammy Davis, Jr., and blues singer Billy Eckstine there in the late '60s.

Drummer boy Hal keeps time for his first rock group. On bongos is Jeff Stern—now my publisher.

It was in this year that I first became aware of the number of incredible singles (I started my collection of 45s this year) and albums out. At this time in my life, I listened to all of my record albums on a tiny portable RCA turntable that my parents gave me for Christmas. I still have it.

For thirty-six years now I have been listening to many of the albums discussed in this chapter and marveling at their brilliance and creativity; I don't think there will ever be a year more influential on the genre of rock music than 1966. The albums all stand the test of time, and many of them have influenced singers and bands of later generations.

BRIAN WILSON ON 1966

In 1966, I was young and happy, and I wrote and created *Pet Sounds* on my piano in collaboration with Tony Asher. Though one might think that prior to 1966 I had an abundance of commercial success, in my heart I felt *Pet Sounds* was my first *real true* musical adventure. I experimented in many ways, instrumentally and vocally, and I knew in my gut that I had a special creation.

Later that year, I created *Good Vibrations*, using six different recording studios and going through many musical and lyrical corrections. Finally, when all was said and sung . . . we all knew we had a great record on our hands. All in all, 1966 was the most creative year of my long and successful career.

1.
PET SOUNDS
(THE BEACH BOYS)

This is the crowning musical achievement of genius Brian Wilson, who spent many months in late '65 and early '66 locked within the confines of recording studios like Gold Star and United Western with many of Phil Spector's "Wrecking Crew" session musicians (notably drummer Hal Blaine and bass player Carol Kaye) fine-tuning every layer of this artistic masterpiece. The other Beach Boys, who were out touring at the time, played mainly a supporting role in this project, but they did many of the trademark backing vocals. The album featured introspective, heartfelt lyrics by Tony Asher and Brian Wilson, set against incredibly sophisticated symphonic music tracks, all written by Brian. It stands up to any other rock album in history as the definitive "concept album." *MOJO* magazine in England would vote *Pet Sounds* the greatest rock album of all time.

Brian said he wanted to make an album as good as the Beatles' *Rubber Soul*, and he surely succeeded. Paul McCartney has often cited *Pet Sounds* as his all-time favorite album and remarked that it influenced him and John Lennon to write and orchestrate *Sgt. Pepper's Lonely Hearts Club Band* with similar effects, like bass harmonica ("Being for the Benefit of Mr. Kite") and three-four-time waltz tempos.

Pet Sounds was released as a box set a few years ago, with all the vocal music tracks isolated, and with studio outtakes and many other extras. The producer of the box set, David Leaf, worked diligently with Brian to create the first-ever stereo mix of the album, and to faithfully restore the original tracks.

This was one of the most memorable albums of my childhood. I remember hearing songs like "Caroline, No" and "Wouldn't It Be Nice" and being mesmerized by the songs' visual imagery. However, I didn't really discover the depth of this music until years later. I am still making new discoveries in *Pet Sounds* every time I listen.

The Beach Boys Pet Sounds

Wouldn't It Be Nice/You Still Believe In Me
That's Not Me/Don't Talk (Put Your Head on My Shoulder)
I'm Waiting For The Day/Let's Go Away For Awhile/Sloop John B.
God Only Knows/I Know There's An Answer/Here Today
I Just Wasn't Made For These Times/Pet Sounds/Caroline No
Plus Bonus Track
Hang On To Your Ego

A few years ago at the Hollywood Bowl, I had the genuine thrill of seeing *Pet Sounds* performed live, in its entirety, by Brian Wilson and his incredible band, with the backing of the Hollywood Bowl orchestra. On "Caroline, No," they even recreated the musical notes that drummer Hal Blaine had originally created by hitting an empty plastic orange-juice bottle with his drumstick. By putting the microphone inside of the bottle, it created a very unique, haunting effect that is one of the trademark sounds on the original recording.

2.
REVOLVER
(THE BEATLES)

This magnificent, innovative, and progressive album was a breakthrough for the Beatles, who in 1966 had reached their creative peak. Every song was incredibly sophisticated and melodic, and had incisive lyrics. Tracks like "Good Day Sunshine," "And Your Bird Can Sing" (used in '66 as one of the theme songs to the Saturday-morning *Beatles* cartoon on ABC), "Tomorrow Never Knows," and "Eleanor Rigby" are true rock masterpieces. Even as a six-year-old, I knew they had something sublimely special going for them. What other group could successfully fuse a Vivaldi string quartet into a pop record?

The cover art on *Revolver* was a truly spectacular photo collage created by Klaus Voorman, who was not only a graphic designer but also a respected session musician on bass guitar. I remember looking at the cover of *Revolver* and feeling that it personified the year 1966. I would listen to this album over and over, and the song "Got to Get You into My Life" was a real favorite also; I loved the Motown-inspired horn section. Another cool piece of trivia: The chorus riff in which George Harrison sings "Taxman!" may have indeed been influenced by the *Batman* theme of this year. . . . Think about it.

I will always cherish the album *Revolver*, as it proved to me as a kid that the Beatles had multiple sonic layers in their music and they raised the standard for many of their competitors. I don't think any rock band has ever topped this album.

REVOLVER

3.
SUPREMES A' GO-GO
(THE SUPREMES)

Wonderful cover art that really captured the carefree, exuberant spirit of '66! I loved this album as a kid. It had the monster singles "Love Is Like an Itching in My Heart" and "You Can't Hurry Love," and great cover versions of "These Boots Are Made for Walking" (with acoustic upright bass, like on Nancy Sinatra's original single) and "Hang On Sloopy" (one of my all-time favorite transistor-radio records, originally recorded in '65 by the McCoys). Mary Wilson shined in a rare solo spotlight on "Come and Get These Memories."

This album really hammered down the quintessential Motown sound (with crack drumming by Benny Benjamin), and it was unceasingly up-tempo and fun. I remember jumping up and down on my bed listening to this album, thinking I might catch the eye of one of the *Hullabaloo* go-go girls on TV.

THE SUPREMES A' GO·GO

LOVE IS LIKE AN ITCHING IN MY HEART □ YOU CAN'T HURRY LOVE □ THIS OLD HEART OF MINE (Is Weak For You) □ SHAKE ME, WAKE ME (When It's Over) □ BABY I NEED YOUR LOVING □ THESE BOOTS ARE MADE FOR WALKING □ I CAN'T HELP MYSELF □ GET READY □ PUT YOURSELF IN MY PLACE □ MONEY (That's What I Want) □ COME AND GET THESE MEMORIES □ HANG ON SLOOPY

MOTOWN

M5-138V1

4.
BLONDE ON BLONDE
(BOB DYLAN)

Bob Dylan was the preeminent songwriter of the 1960s. This double-album masterpiece served as my first comprehensive introduction to his music. My older teen neighbor David Cohen always had it playing on his portable General Electric stereo with detachable speakers.

The big standouts for me are songs like "Just Like a Woman," "Rainy Day Women #12 & 35," the electric rocker "Leopard-Skin Pill-Box Hat," and, of course, the majestic country-rock "I Want You." This album contained material that was much more accessible to me as a young listener than earlier Dylan songs had been, and hits like "Just Like a Woman" and "I Want You" made it into the *Billboard* Top Forty.

The magic was in the whole presentation; this album brought a new dimension to the folk rock genre. *Blonde on Blonde* took it a step further than the Byrds had in 1965 for "Mr. Tambourine Man," when they set Dylan's music to a rock beat courtesy of Roger McGuinn's twelve-string electric Rickenbacker guitar. Recording *Blonde on Blonde* in Nashville, Dylan created a tapestry of musical styles ranging from folk to blues and even gospel.

Bob Dylan was in the midst of his rock music renaissance in '66, and, on July 29 of this year, he ended the first phase of his career by crashing his motorcycle on a country road near Woodstock, New York. His lengthy recovery period added even more mystique to his already cloudy image.

Dylan was a complex artist in the '60s—he really wrote poetry set to music. So I could not fully appreciate his music until years later, when the nuances and idiosyncrasies of his storytelling made more sense to me. The words were always hard to decipher, but the feeling and the rhythm were there, and I knew his music was extremely vital and soulful. This album defines a generation and it was a true highlight of the year for me.

5.
GOT LIVE IF YOU WANT IT!
(THE ROLLING STONES)

This was one of the first albums my parents ever bought for me. It was the Rolling Stones' first live album, and I was thrilled to hear it in my bedroom while reading through my *Tiger Beat* magazines. This record had so many of the group's hit songs on it: "Under My Thumb," "Not Fade Away," "Get Off of My Cloud," and "19th Nervous Breakdown." It was recorded at the Royal Albert Hall, which I had heard about in connection with the Beatles performing there, so I knew it was a prestigious venue. I loved the cover of this album, too, with all the "action poses" of Mick Jagger and the guys onstage.

The pulse of this album was so frenetic and exciting. It was like having the Stones fly into the Valley and do a private concert for me. Sometimes, to create a real "concert setting," I would turn out the big light in my room and turn on a pole lamp in the corner that had three individual spotlights on it. I would play along to the album on my little drum kit and pretend I was Charlie Watts, the Stones' drummer. Actually, I remember drumming to the Stones song "Satisfaction" in 1965, before I even had any real drums to play. I would put my Frisbee on top of a trashcan and use that, along with maybe a soup kettle or two.

I really loved one song on this disc, "Fortune Teller." I had never heard it on the radio before, and I thought the idea of a guy marrying a fortune teller (and then getting his fortunes told for free) was really intriguing. This song reminded me of "Love Potion Number Nine" by the Searchers (1965). I also liked that Mick Jagger sang the hit songs on this LP a little differently than on the singles. This album made a very personal impression on me, and grew on me as I got older. (I would love 1970's *Get Yer Ya-Ya's Out*, too . . . especially the cover shot of Charlie Watts in a top hat jumping jubilantly into the air beside a burro saddled up with his Gretsch drum set.)

The Stones had a harder edge than the Beatles, and a much tougher, more blues-inspired sound than the Beatles or more pop-oriented British Invasion groups like Chad and Jeremy or Herman's Hermits. (However, British groups like the Animals and the Yardbirds also employed the razor-edged blues beat of the Stones.) *Got Live . . .* is a smashing example of how mesmerizing the Stones could be in live performance. Amazingly, that ability has remained to this day, as the Stones prepare for their 2002 World Tour.

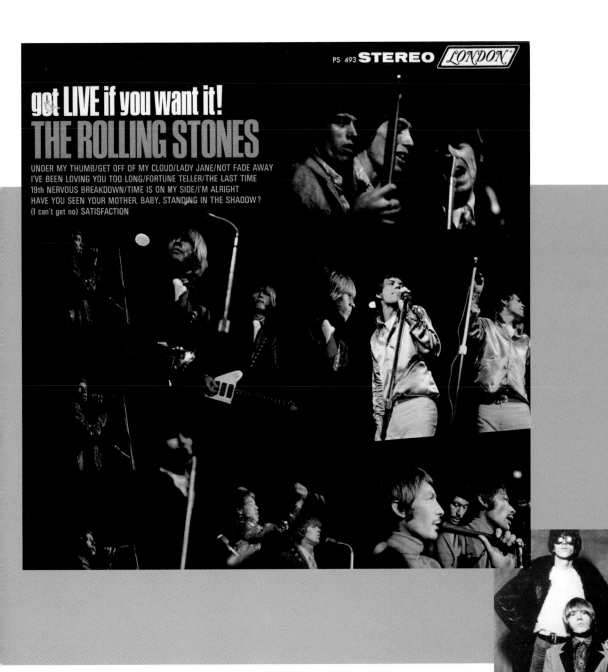

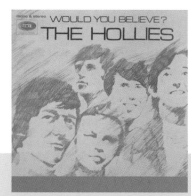

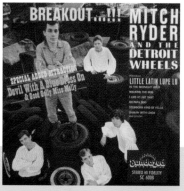

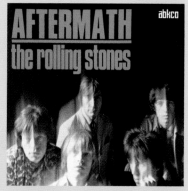

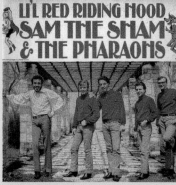

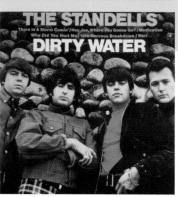

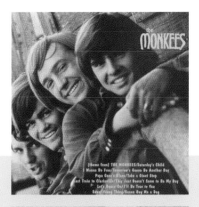

When the Monkees' debut album came out in the fall of '66, every kid in my neighborhood had a copy. Micky Dolenz and Davy Jones handled most of the lead vocal work on the self-titled LP; my favorite songs were "Take a Giant Step" and "I Wanna Be Free." "Gonna Buy Me a Dog" exemplified the comedic flavor of the Monkees. Earlier in '66 their first single, "Last Train to Clarksville," had gone to number one right out of the gate. (The song was written by Tommy Boyce and Bobby Hart, who produced and provided backup vocals for the group.) Later in the year their second single, "I'm a Believer" (written by Neil Diamond), also went to number one.

If You Can Believe Your Eyes and Ears was the outstanding first album of the Mamas and the Papas, Greenwich Village folkies who moved west to electrify their sound. Living in L.A.'s famed Laurel Canyon, John and Michelle Phillips, Denny Doherty, and Mama Cass Elliot performed beautiful, sun-drenched harmonies under the guidance of producer Lou Adler. "California Dreamin'" became a reality, as their first single shot to number four on the *Billboard* chart. Their second single from this album, "Monday Monday," went to number one; it exemplified the group's wistful but joyous musical style. Their song "Straight Shooter" was a favorite of mine; it reminded me of the Lone Ranger.

Simon and Garfunkel's folk rock classic *Sounds of Silence* was released in early '66, on the heels of the number-one title song. Poignant harpsichord on "Leaves That Are Green," and the powerful alienation of "I Am a Rock" and "Richard Cory" established the singers as rock poet visionaries. "April Come She Will" and "The Sounds of Silence" were later used in the film *The Graduate* (1967), where they played pivotal roles in defining the identity crisis of Dustin Hoffman's character.

This year the Byrds released their masterwork *Fifth Dimension*, their foray into psychedelic space rock, and their first album without a Dylan song. The title track ("5D") and "Eight Miles High" showed that group leader Roger McGuinn was developing a true sense of the avant garde; his daring, jazz-inspired musical arrangements transcended the more acoustic sound for which the group was known. "Mr. Spaceman" was a fave, with its jaunty country flavor. The harmonies of McGuinn, David Crosby, and new member Chris Hillman, layered against adventurous lyrics, made *Fifth Dimension* a trippy wonder.

In 1966, everyone in Los Angeles was tuned in to one local radio station: 93 KHJ, Boss Radio. The station had kicked off in April of 1965, and by '66 it had already become the biggest thing on the radio since the antennae. Unbelievably cool "Boss Jocks" like Sam Riddle, Humble Harve, Robert W. Morgan, and my hero, the Real Don Steele, played a Top Forty format (actually, it was the "Boss Thirty") that featured pop, rock, soul, and easy listening. The great variety of musical genres dazzled my young mind.

BOSS HIT BOUNDS

FLAMINGO
Herb Alpert & The Tijuana Brass   A & M
LAST TRAIN TO CLARKSVILLE
The Monkees   Colgems
I CHOSE TO SING THE BLUES
Ray Charles   ABC

WIN CASH!
play
TIME BOMB
on
93/KHJ
BOSS RADIO
IN LOS ANGELES

BOSS 30
FROM 93/KHJ

Hear THE REAL DON STEELE on 93/KHJ 3-6 pm

BOSS

GOD ONLY KNOWS
Beach Boys   Capitol
ALFIE
Cher   Imperial
OUTSIDE CHANCE
The Turtles   White Whale

YOU CAN WIN THE $8,000
COBRA-POWERED
KHJ SURFIN' BIRD

BUILT FOR THE BIG KAHUNA BY BILL CUSHENBERRY! CALL THE BOSSLINE AT THE SOUND OF THE COCKATOO ...AND WIN ONE OF THE KAHUNA'S TIKI CHARMS...THEN YOU'RE IN THE RUNNING TO COP THE CAR OF THE YEAR FROM...

93/KHJ
BOSS RADIO
IN LOS ANGELES

BOSS 30
FROM 93/KHJ

Hear THE REAL DON STEELE on 93/KHJ 3-6 pm

The Real Don Steele and Jackie DeShannon.

The Fabulous Ventures! They released all three of these classic albums in '66, and each of them was spectacular. On the *Batman* album they performed "Secret Agent Man," the theme from *Get Smart*, and a vicious version of the TV Bat-theme. Also on this album were signature Ventures originals—like "The Cape," "Joker's Wild," and "007-11"—which featured awesome spy guitar and *Batman*-inspired effects, including mysterious background vocals. I would use this album as the soundtrack when playing *Batman* with my buddies. Great background music for capturing arch-villains and staging mock Bat-fights, which included jumping off my bed into the melee.

Wild Things! featured fat and nasty fuzz guitars—the original compositions "Fuzzy and Wild" and "Wild Child" were wicked cool. The album *Go with the Ventures!* featured "Eight Miles High," "These Boots Are Made for Walkin'," and the number-one Japanese hit "Ginza Lights."

The Ventures recorded dozens of albums in the '60s, but these are three of my all-time faves. Drummer Mel Taylor was one of the best rock drummers ever!

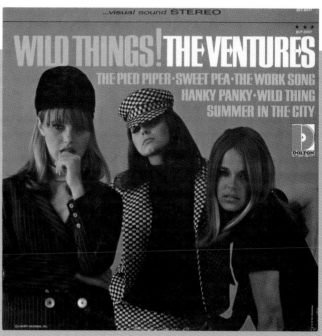

YOU BABY
THE TURTLES
LET ME BE

WHITE WHALE

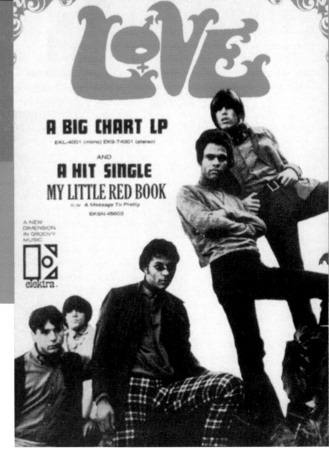

SENSATIONAL, HIGHLY UNDERRATED BAND OF '66: LOVE Arthur Lee and his band Love captivated audiences with their blistering live shows at the Whisky A Go Go and Bido Lito's in '66. The Doors worshipped them and were their opening act this year. Love's big hits "My Little Red Book" and "7 and 7 Is" were pulsating slammers, but the band really shined in intricate, often baroque pop ballads that used mariachi horns and lush strings. Due to Arthur's resistance to touring and his mercurial persona, the band never found the success it deserved—except in the U.K., where they are still revered. Our Japanese housekeeper, Kiku, got me interested in this group a few years later, in the summer of '69. In 2002, Arthur Lee resurfaced with a new version of Love.

In '66, soul music took some big strides. The classic Motown sound was still popular, but I also dug the heavy beat of the Memphis soul singers and groups on the Stax label, notably Otis Redding and Booker T. and the MGs. As I began to pursue my interest in drumming this year, I loved playing along to Otis Redding's "I Can't Turn You Loose" and "Mr. Pitiful" from his hard-driving live album. Otis Redding was backed by Booker T. and the MGs on many of his records, including his masterpiece *The Dictionary of Soul*, which featured my favorite tracks "Sweet Lorene" and "Try a Little Tenderness." The drumming of Al Jackson, Jr., and the bass playing of Donald "Duck" Dunn sent me through the roof!

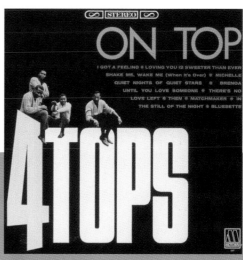

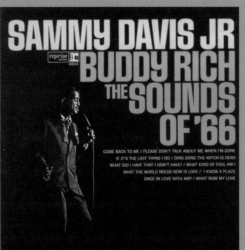

Pop music was very much a part of Top Forty radio in '66. As kids, we were exposed to this more "adult" music on our radio stations, so it seemed cool, but it was also featured on many of the TV variety shows and used as filler music on the local news or when the TV channel went dark with technical difficulties. (I remember one group whose music was used quite heavily for this purpose: Sergio Mendes and Brasil '66, whose debut album appeared this year.)

Herb Alpert and the Tijuana Brass was a major musical force in my childhood, and when I hear this music today it takes me right back into my happiest memories of the '60s. In 1965, the classic albums

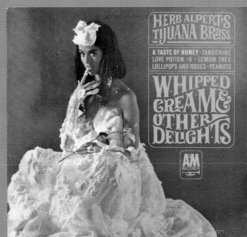

Whipped Cream and Other Delights and Going Places were released; they were played heavily into 1966. Songs like "Whipped Cream" (used on The Dating Game) and "Tijuana Taxi" came from these albums. After seeing the now legendary cover of the Whipped Cream LP, I would never look at a carton of Cool Whip the same way!

In 1966 Herb Alpert released What Now My Love, which contained the infectious songs "Magic Trumpet," "Plucky," and "Freckles." Whenever I heard the music of Herb Alpert as a kid, I always felt happy. It was the most uplifting experience to hear it (and it remains so even to this day). The melodies of the songs were so catchy; I loved the sound of the marimbas and mariachi horns. It made me want to visit Spain and dress like a matador. The best I could do was watch Zorro reruns and wave a red bath towel around while my brother charged at me.

87

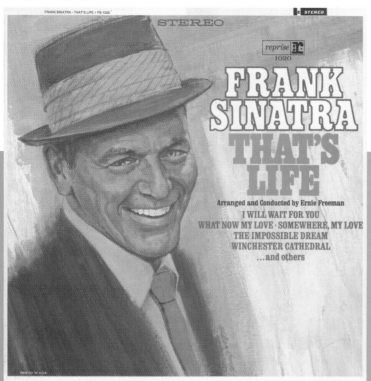

STEREO

reprise 1020

FRANK SINATRA
THAT'S LIFE

Arranged and Conducted by Ernie Freeman

I WILL WAIT FOR YOU
WHAT NOW MY LOVE · SOMEWHERE, MY LOVE
THE IMPOSSIBLE DREAM
WINCHESTER CATHEDRAL
...and others

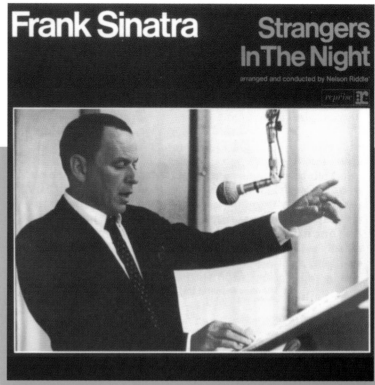

Frank Sinatra   **Strangers In The Night**

arranged and conducted by Nelson Riddle

reprise

MOONLIGHT SINATRA

arranged and conducted by NELSON RIDDLE

MOONLIGHT BECOMES YOU / MOON SONG / MOONLIGHT
SERENADE / REACHING FOR THE MOON /
I WISHED ON THE MOON / OH, YOU
CRAZY MOON / THE MOON GOT IN
MY EYES / MOONLIGHT MOOD /
MOON LOVE / THE MOON
WAS YELLOW
(And The Night
Was Young)

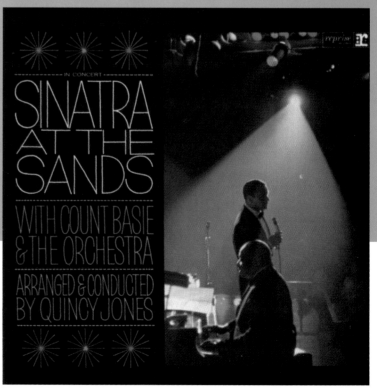

reprise

IN CONCERT

SINATRA AT THE SANDS

WITH COUNT BASIE & THE ORCHESTRA

ARRANGED & CONDUCTED BY QUINCY JONES

Frank Sinatra released four albums in '66, while daughter Nancy had three. Frank went to number one on the *Billboard* pop charts for the first time in the '60s with the single "Strangers in the Night." "That's Life" went to number four. His live album, *Sinatra at the Sands*, was recorded in early '66, with the Count Basie orchestra and arrangements by Quincy Jones. (This was the first re-teaming of these three musical giants since the masterpiece 1964 album *It Might As Well Be Swing*, on which "Fly Me to the Moon" appeared.)

I remember my dad playing *Sinatra at the Sands* on the hi-fi in the den, exposing me at a young age to the timeless swing of Frank and the boys. The album opens with a sizzling version of "Come Fly with Me" and doesn't rest until Frank does his monologue near the end of the album. This double LP made me feel like I was right there in the showroom at the Sands Hotel. I wanted to be cavorting with the Rat Pack at this point in my life, but instead I had to settle for taking care of my two hamsters. Sinatra runs through many of his hit songs on this album, and "My Kind of Town" really wails. Unbelievably swingin' drumming by Sonny Payne.

Nancy Sinatra released her first album in early '66: the smash hit *Boots*. It included hip cover versions of the Beatles' "Run for Your Life" and Dylan's "It Ain't Me Babe." Two other albums followed this year: the *Boots* sequel *How Does That Grab You?* and *Nancy in London*. Nancy proved her tremendous versatility as an artist with her first three LP releases. Her music was extremely well produced by Lee Hazlewood, and it had a grown-up quality which, even as a kid, I really enjoyed.

Nancy's voice was what stood out to me; it was warm and friendly, yet tough-talking and contemptuous when it needed to be. Her independent image was both unique and irresistible, and I remember insisting my parents buy me her *Boots* album at Fedco, a pre-Costco discount store. I played it many times at the record parties I had with my friends, and Nancy's version of "Day Tripper" knocked me out!

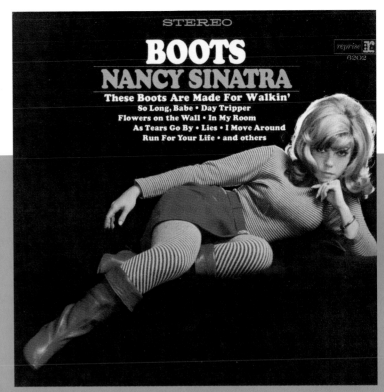

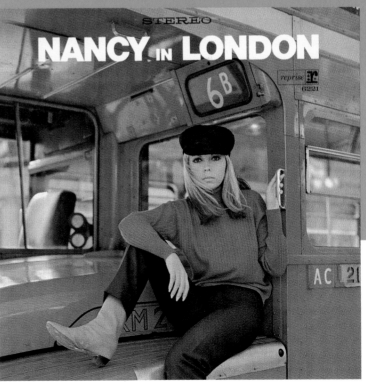

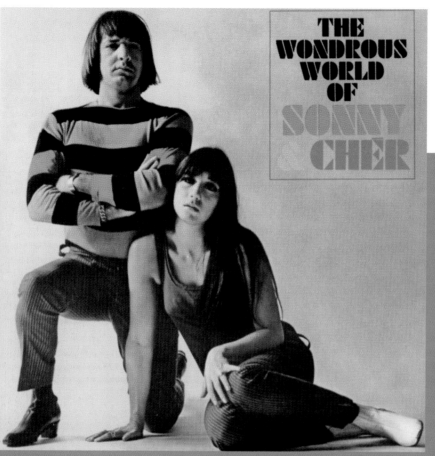

THE WONDROUS WORLD OF SONNY & CHER

Other than Batman and Robin, Sonny and Cher were the most dynamic duo of 1966. Their breakthrough hit had come the year before, with "I Got You Babe" (number one in July of '65), and it was followed by the re-charting of their 1964 record "Baby Don't Go." Their quirky personalities and hippie wardrobe made them instant '60s icons. I always wanted a mock animal vest like Sonny wore.

The two had worked as backup singers for Phil Spector, and Sonny modeled his production style after his mentor's, and used many of the same musicians. "I Got You Babe" had the lush orchestration of many of Phil Spector's biggest hits. It even featured an oboe solo as the key musical "hook."

In 1966, Sonny and Cher released their second album, *The Wondrous World of Sonny and Cher*. Excellent cover versions of the Kinks' "Set Me Free," the Zombies' "Leave Me Be," and "What Now My Love," which made it to number fourteen in January of '66. (Frank Sinatra had a great recording of this tune on his *That's Life* album.) Cher really put the pedal to the floor on her rendition of "Summertime," the Gershwin tune that R&B singer Billy Stewart had a big hit with in July of '66.

SONNY & CHER'S FASHION-ABLE CONTEST

DO SONNY and CHER look TOO WAY-OUT?

Get in on the "Gravy Train" of Prizes! Prizes! Prizes! 29 of em...

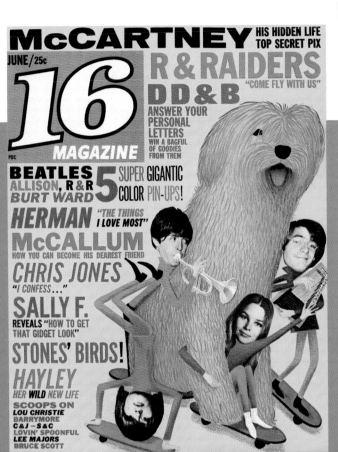

McCARTNEY HIS HIDDEN LIFE TOP SECRET PIX

JUNE/25¢

16 MAGAZINE

PDC

R & RAIDERS
DD&B
"COME FLY WITH US"

ANSWER YOUR PERSONAL LETTERS
WIN A BAGFUL OF GOODIES FROM THEM

5 SUPER COLOR GIGANTIC PIN-UPS!

BEATLES ALLISON, R&R BURT WARD

HERMAN "THE THINGS I LOVE MOST"

McCALLUM
HOW YOU CAN BECOME HIS DEAREST FRIEND

CHRIS JONES "I CONFESS..."

SALLY F. REVEALS "HOW TO GET THAT GIDGET LOOK"

STONES' BIRDS!

HAYLEY HER WILD NEW LIFE

SCOOPS ON
LOU CHRISTIE
BARRYMORE
C&J – S&C
LOVIN' SPOONFUL
LEE MAJORS
BRUCE SCOTT

HERMAN'S MUM REVEALS HIS TRUE LIFE AND LUVS

go go with Teen Life

Apr. 25¢

DINO, DESI and BILLY

4 BIG CONTESTS! 400 VALUABLE PRIZES!

SECRETS BEHIND HAYLEY'S BITTER-SWEET MEMORIES About Boys, Her Parents and Her Nightmares

LUKE'S FAB SURPRISE!

ELVIS: SWINGER in PARADISE

Heather North: A TEENAGER LOOKS AT SEX

PAUL McCARTNEY LIFE STORY IN PIX

SALLY FIELD: GET THE BOY YOU WANT!

ADVENTURES OF TEENA A GO GO

Exclusive! HEARTBREAK LIFE OF EX-BEATLE PETER BEST

I know there will never be a better musical decade than the 1960s. I am so thankful I got to be a kid during this revolutionary period in rock music. Every weekend I would look forward to watching the teen music shows on TV, which brought to life both the songs and dance moves of the day and made me really look forward to growing up. Who would've thought that, all these years later, this one year in pop music would remain the standard of excellence to which I compare all other periods? Throughout 1966 I kept the beat on my gold-sparkle-finish drum kit and, to this day, I still feel the wondrous rhythms in my soul when listening to the sounds of '66.

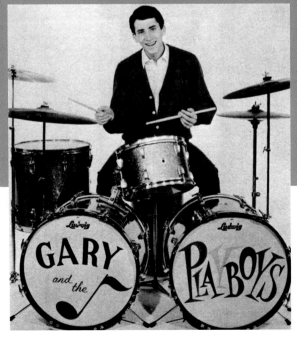

BILLBOARD NUMBER-ONE SINGLES OF 1966

1) "The Sounds of Silence" (Simon and Garfunkel)
2) "We Can Work It Out" (The Beatles)
3) "My Love" (Petula Clark)
4) "Lightnin' Strikes" (Lou Christie)
5) "These Boots Are Made for Walkin'" (Nancy Sinatra)
6) "The Ballad of the Green Berets" (Sgt. Barry Sadler)
7) "Good Lovin'" (The Young Rascals)
8) "Monday Monday" (The Mamas and the Papas)
9) "When a Man Loves a Woman" (Percy Sledge)
10) "Paint It Black" (The Rolling Stones)
11) "Paperback Writer" (The Beatles)
12) "Strangers in the Night" (Frank Sinatra)
13) "Hanky Panky" (Tommy James and the Shondells)
14) "Wild Thing" (The Troggs)
15) "Summer in the City" (The Lovin' Spoonful)
16) "Sunshine Superman" (Donovan)
17) "You Can't Hurry Love" (The Supremes)
18) "Cherish" (The Association)
19) "Reach Out I'll Be There" (The Four Tops)

BILLBOARD TOP TEN SINGLES:
WEEK ENDING JULY 16, 1966
(MY SIXTH BIRTHDAY)

1) "Hanky Panky" (Tommy James and the Shondells)
2) "Wild Thing" (The Troggs)
3) "Red Rubber Ball" (The Cyrkle)
4) "You Don't Have to Say You Love Me" (Dusty Springfield)
5) "Paperback Writer" (The Beatles)
6) "Strangers in the Night" (Frank Sinatra)
7) "Along Comes Mary" (The Association)
8) "Little Girl" (Syndicate of Sound)
9) "Lil' Red Riding Hood" (Sam the Sham and the Pharaohs)
10) "Hungry" (Paul Revere and the Raiders)

BILLBOARD TOP TEN SINGLES:
WEEK ENDING DECEMBER 31, 1966

1) "I'm a Believer" (The Monkees)
2) "Snoopy vs. the Red Baron" (The Royal Guardsmen)
3) "Winchester Cathedral" (The New Vaudeville Band)
4) "That's Life" (Frank Sinatra)
5) "Sugar Town" (Nancy Sinatra)
6) "Mellow Yellow " (Donovan)
7) "Tell It Like It Is" (Aaron Neville)
8) "(I Know) I'm Losing You" (The Temptations)
9) "A Place in the Sun" (Stevie Wonder)
10) "Good Thing" (Paul Revere and the Raiders)

4 PLAYTIME

The highlight of my childhood experience in 1966 was playing with the wonderful and clever toys that were given to me for my birthday, Chanukah, Christmas, and for occasional bouts of good behavior. Actually, some of my favorite toys in this year were very inexpensive items that my mom purchased for me at the grocery store. Scientific wonders like the Whee-Lo and the Monster Magnet brought hours of fun and enchantment. I remember using the red plastic Monster Magnet to lift up our metal card-table chairs, and making it defy gravity by sticking it sideways to our refrigerator door.

Eventually, I received an allowance and stored the funds in my treasured Batman wallet, which contained a plastic coin holder and a little magic slate on which I could write secret messages or the combination to my bike lock.

Back in the day, a few early toys were especially precious to me: my first Gumby doll (by Lakeside), my Green Hornet Super-Flex doll (similar to Gumby), my Tickle Bee game, and, of course, every kid's first board game, Candy Land, which I would play for hours at a time. To this day, when I see images of the Peanut Brittle House, the Gumdrop Mountains, and the Lollipop Woods, I'm still transported to that magical land—a place similar to where I imagined the Pied Piper was leading the children of Hamelin.

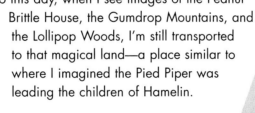

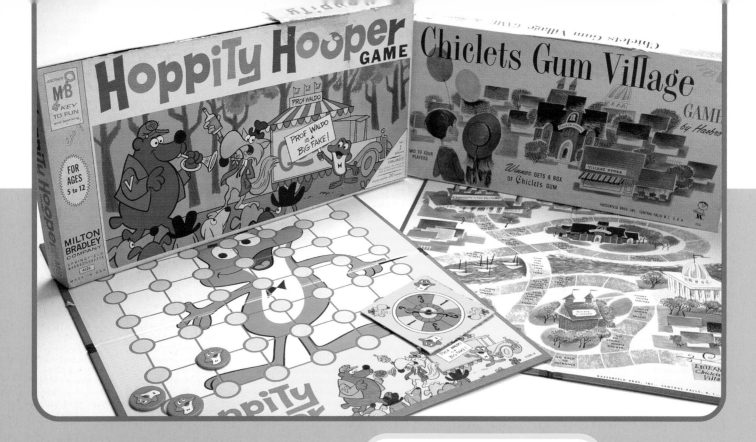

The Chiclets board game was an obvious Candy Land knockoff, and it's now quite rare. Also seen here is my Hoppity Hooper board game; it featured my pals from my favorite Jay Ward cartoon, which had debuted two years earlier but was still on TV in '66.

Frosty the Sno-Cone Maker was one of my absolute favorite toys, not just of '66, but of the entire decade. The notion that I could create homemade sno-cones during the hot Valley summers was both refreshing and innovative. You would push the ice cube down using Frosty's hat and then crank the lever on his back, and crushed ice would fall out of his chest. I remember using Mom's funnel to fill the little plastic squeeze bottles with Hi-C and Kool Aid, and using Frosty's little shovel to pat down the ice on my jumbo-size "Suicide" sno-cone—which had squirts of all the different flavors on it.

Wham-O was undoubtedly the coolest and most creative toy company of the entire decade. In the late '50s and early '60s, Wham-O had created a sensation with the Hula Hoop, and then with dazzling fluorescent yo-yos. The next big invention from Wham-O was the Super Ball; powered by a space-age rubber compound called Zectron, it supposedly contained fifty thousand pounds of compressed energy. This enabled me to bounce my Super Ball right over the house. Unfortunately, after it landed in the ivy, I was back to playing with my Slinky. (Fortunately, less expensive Super Mini-Balls popped up—in psychedelic swirl colors.)

In 1966, Wham-O introduced Super Stuff, much to the chagrin of parents with shag carpeting. This hot pink, gooey concoction had a minty scent, and reminded me of the Blob from the 1958 drive-in classic.

I also loved hooking up my treasured Water Wiggle to the family garden hose and watching his funny orange head fly around the yard with more kinetic energy than my brother Bob after eating three packs of Sugar Babies. Water Wiggle had a special charm, kind of like a crazy sea serpent from which we had to escape while running through the sprinklers.

97

NEW   **TWISTER**™   For 2 to 4 Players

THE GAME THAT TIES YOU UP IN KNOTS
Twister

Ages: 8 to Adult

It's the new "stockin' feet"™ game sensation that's fun for everyone — youngsters, teens and adults. Twister puts two players face-to-face in a fantastically funny test of pretzel-ability. Each spin requires players to move a hand or foot into a different colored circle on the vinyl game rug. As the players move into each other, it becomes harder and harder to stay in balance and still find room for hands and feet. First one to topple is the loser! An indoor or outdoor game.

CONTAINS: Large-size washable vinyl game rug, giant spinner with plastic arrow. Box size: 18¼" x 13½".

No. 4645
Retail: $5.00

Ctn. Quan. 6
Ctn. Wt. 18 lbs.

ANOTHER
MB
KEY
TO FUN
and learning
®

FOR
ALL
AGES

BOARD GAMES ... PAGES 1 THROUGH 30

CARD GAMES ... PAGES 31 THROUGH 40

SKILL & ACTION GAMES ... PAGES 41 THROUGH 50

ARTS & ACTIVITIES ... PAGES 51 THROUGH 56

PUZZLES FOR ALL AGES ... PAGES 57 THROUGH 72

MILTON BRADLEY COMPANY
SPRINGFIELD MASSACHUSETTS

1966 GAMES CATALOG

With the notable exception of Monopoly from Parker Brothers, most of the classic board games of my childhood were manufactured by Milton Bradley. In 1966 they introduced Twister, which borrowed the foot maps used in dance studios and created a gymnastics free-for-all that usually led to some kind of a wrestling match between my pals and me. I've often thought of marketing a Twister bedspread and spinner-embossed headboard. I think it might really catch on. . . .

JAMES BOND THUNDERBALL GAME

For 2 to 4 Players

Ages: 10 to Adult

This suspense-filled game closely follows the action of the exciting 007 film adventure, "THUNDERBALL". Players must first locate, then capture, a hidden atom bomb. The intrigue mounts as each player attempts to gather all the clues necessary to find the bomb, using devious routes to hide his progress and the "Spectre" agent to delay opposing players.

CONTAINS: 5 playing pieces on plastic bases, 6 bombs, 7 letter-pieces spelling "Spectre", 6 area markers, 6 decoder notebooks and a pair of dice. Box size: 19" x 9½".

Ctn. Quan. 12
Ctn. Wt. 25 lbs.

No. 4547
Retail: $3.00

NEW

JAMES BOND GOLDFINGER GAME

For 2 Players

Ages: 10 to Adult

007 and Goldfinger are at it again in this fascinating 2 player game. The player who is Goldfinger uses his henchmen and his wits to escape from the Fort Knox game-board. 007 and his support forces must trap Goldfinger on the board to win the game.

CONTAINS: Colorful playing board which is a replica of Fort Knox vaults, 16 plastic James Bond Agents and 8 Goldfinger "henchmen" plus Goldfinger himself. Box size: 19" x 9½".

Ctn. Quan. 12
Ctn. Wt. 21 lbs.

No. 4635
Retail: $3.00

JAMES BOND SECRET AGENT 007 GAME

For 2 to 4 Players

Ages: 10 to Adult

On a game-board of mystery and intrigue, players are all secret agents working against their opponents to rendezvous with friendly agents. Timing is vitally important because scores are based on the position of the clock. As the game progresses, double and triple scores are possible for the strategist who can rendezvous several agents without being frustrated by his opponents.

CONTAINS: 16 plastic "agent" playing pieces in 4 colors, rendezvous cards, score markers and clock dial scorer. Box size: 19" x 9½".

Ctn. Quan. 12
Ctn. Wt. 21 lbs.

No. 4527
Retail: $2.00

MYSTERY DATE

For 2 to 4 Players

Ages: 8 to 16

For Girls Only. Players travel around the colorful playing board, trying to collect the right combination of cards to complete their date-time outfits. The girl who has the right combination of cards gets to open the mystery door and meet her mystery date, but she must be wearing the proper attire for that particular beau in order to win the game. There are four mystery dates and no one knows who will come calling. There is an element of risk, for one of the mystery dates is the "pest", the date that no one wants.

CONTAINS: A full color 18" x 13" game board which has an attached plastic mystery door that opens to reveal the mystery date. 48 full color playing cards showing 16 glamorous outfits and 4 "Girl" playing PIECES ON PLASTIC STANDS. Box size 18¼" x 13½".

Ctn. Quan. 12
Ctn. Wt. 22 lbs.

No. 4502
Retail $3.00

NEW

BATMAN

For 2 to 4 Players

Ages: 8 to 15

Here's a game-board adventure featuring that dynamic duo of TV and the Comics, Batman and Robin. Players are all citizens of Gotham City caught up in a crime wave of dastardly villains like the "Riddler" and "Mr. Freeze". Each player uses the Batmobile and his Batcontrol board trying to capture six different criminals and win the game.

CONTAINS: Action-illustrated playing board, 4 plastic playing pieces, 3 plastic Batmobiles, 5 each of 6 villain pieces, 6 super crime labs and one die. Box size: 19" x 9½".

Ctn. Quan. 12
Ctn. Wt. 22 lbs.

No. 4648
Retail: $3.00

DIAL 'N SPELL*

For 1 player

Ages: 4 to 8

This is a really different word game for eager youngsters. Every child enjoys using a telephone — here he spells words by dialing letters. The words are names of objects that are shown around the dial. When a word is spelled correctly, an arrow on the dial points to the object. Helps build vocabulary while the child enjoys "playing telephone". Box size 9½"x19".

CONTAINS: Plastic telephone dial 4½" in diameter, mounted on 9" square cardboard base colorfully illustrated with 9 objects a child sees in the world around him; plus 5 additional cards similarly illustrated on both sides, providing a total of 99 different words and objects. Box size 19" x 9½".

Ctn. Quan. 12
Ctn. Wt. 14 lbs.

No. 4223
Retail: $2.00

MATTEL TOYS 1966

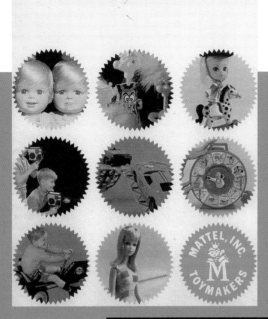

NEW! *Francie*™
BARBIE'S® 'MOD'ERN COUSIN

SHE'S IN!
SHE'S WITH IT!
SHE SWINGS!

FRANCIE™ BARBIE'S® 'MOD'ERN COUSIN WITH
LIFELIKE BENDABLE LEGS AND ROOTED EYELASHES
#1130
FRANCIE opens up the swinging teenage "mod" world.
She has available a vivid-color "mod" wardrobe designed especially
for her attractive young teenage figure. She can also dress
in BARBIE'S costumes. Two hair colors — blonde or brunette
(eyelashes are brunette only). 11¼" tall. With one-piece swimsuit,
shoes and wire stand. Double strength see-through box,
12¾"x4⅛"x2½".
Std. Pack: 1 Doz. Wt: 7½ Lbs.

FRANCIE, BARBIE'S 'MOD'ERN COUSIN
#1140
Standard FRANCIE, as above but without bendable legs or
eyelashes. Two-piece swimsuit.
Std. Pack: 1 Doz. Wt: 8 Lbs.
"FRANCIE" is the trademark of Mattel, Inc., for its DOLL.

Exclusive! Long rooted eyelashes . . .
and eyelash brush.

NEW! THINGMAKER™ FEATURING CREEPLE PEEPLE™

HOLDING COLLARS

MAKE HILARIOUS, LOVEABLE MONSTERS TO DECORATE PENCILS!
#4482
CREEPLE PEEPLE are monstrous — but nice! They're fun to make, fun to play
with! Form fanciful, whimsical CREEPLE PEEPLE in 4 glowing colors
(pink, blue, green, and orange) by pouring special fluorescent PLASTIGOOP™
into metal molds, then heating on the THINGMAKER. Decorate 'em with
colorful wigs, beady eyes, costumes and
feathers. Molds make six different starting
heads, arms and hands, feet-stand for desk or
dresser decoration, tongue, pipe, bug, and a
collar to fasten heads to a pencil or dowel.
Also contains pencils, pencil clips, wear
CREEPLE PEEPLE like jewelry(!) latex-type
paper for costumes and "accessories" (hat,
tongue, chest and padlock, snake), beads for
eyes, wool wigs, feathers. Water tray, mold
handle, removing tool, instructions.
Styrofoam tray storage package.
14¼ x 12¾ x 3¾".
Std. Pack: 6/12 Doz. Wt: 22½ Lbs.

GLOWING
PLASTIGOOP

WACKY HEADS

FEET-STANDS

Aside from Wham-O, Mattel was by far the
most innovative toy manufacturer. Having
created the Barbie doll in 1959 and the
Creepy Crawlers make-your-own-model set
(complete with Thingmaker oven) in 1964,
Mattel was way ahead of the competition.
In '66 they introduced Barbie's mod cousin
Francie and her Carnaby Street wardrobe.
Mattel also expanded the Thingmaker do-it-
yourself line with the introduction of
Creeple Peeple and Fright Factory, which
allowed my brother and me to create our
own rubber vampire fangs, clawed

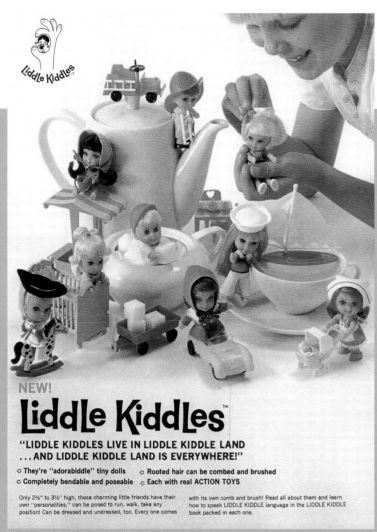

fingernails, and eerie eyeball patches. One of the coolest toys from Mattel this year was the V-RROOM! Motor for your Sting-Ray handlebars, which made the bike sound like a motorcycle. I never got one for my birthday, so I had to settle for the playing-cards-and-clothespin-on-my-spokes routine—which never sounded like an engine but, instead, like I was standing next to the blackjack table in Vegas waiting for my dad to win back my allowance money!

HASBRO

HARVEST OF SPRING TOYS · 1966

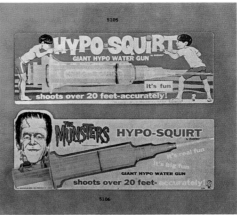

#5105 HYPO-SQUIRT
Here's a fun-filled water toy that tests accuracy and skill. Giant 15" hypodermic water gun made of clear plastic shoots over 20 feet accurately. Contains: ring, tip, nozzle, plunger and tube. Held on card with two wire ties.
Size 23" x 17¼" x 8¼"   2 DOZ.   10 LBS.

#5106 MUNSTERS HYPO-SQUIRT
Hasbro's exclusive fun-filled water toy that tests skill and accuracy. Giant 15" hypodermic water gun made of luminous orange plastic shoots over 20 feet accurately. Contains: ring, tube, nozzle, plunger and tube. Held on card with two wire ties.
Size 23" x 17¼" x 8¼"   2 DOZ.   10 LBS.

#5100 TOP-A-GO-GO
Fantastic 3-way wonder spinning top. It's a top—it's a yo-yo—it's a gyro. Kids can easily master any of 65 different tricks. Made of rugged styrene plastic, with precision machine-tooled metal spindle for gyro action. Comes with molded tops (2 halves) stand, stand insert, 2 handles, yo-yo string. Instructions included.
Size 10½" x 5"   2 DOZ.   8 LBS.

#5110 FLYING SUPERMAN
It's a bird, it's a plane—no it's Flying Superman. Ten inch plastic Superman figure with brilliant red cape. Ruggedly constructed for rugged performance. Comes with sling to launch Superman on his way.
Size 12½" x 9½"   2 DOZ.   8 LBS.

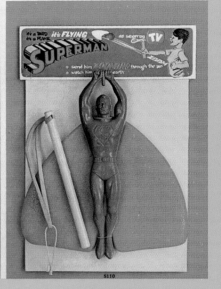

Hasbro was the offbeat toy company that produced Mr. Potato Head. By 1966 Mr. Potato Head had several pals, two of whom were in my collection: Pete the Pepper and Cooky the Cucumber. (The little eyes and nosepieces would always get lost and get sucked up by the vacuum cleaner.) Hasbro also made the wondrous Stardust art kits, with which you would pour tubes of pixie dust into a paint-by-numbers design and end up with "velvet art" suitable for framing. Also out this year was the Munsters Hypo-Squirt toy with Herman's head on the package, now considered to be the rarest of Munsters collectibles. (A friend of mine recently purchased one of these on eBay for over ten thousand dollars!)

Mr. Potato Head and his Tooty Frooty Friends

#2050 PETE THE PEPPER
Here's Pete the Pepper and his friend Mr. Potato Head ready to take shape before your eyes. Life-like vegetables to change into funny, loveable friends. Contains plastic pepper and potato, facial and body parts. Over 30 pieces in all. Instructions included. Size 9" x 6" x 3". 2 DOZ. 12 LBS.

#2051 OSCAR THE ORANGE
Oscar the Orange and his friend Mr. Potato Head are very busy. Assemble and change these life-like fruits and vegetables into funny, loveable friends. Plastic orange and potato, facial and body parts—over 30 pieces to change these lifelike vegetables into funny, loveable friends. Instructions included. Size 9" x 6" x 3". 2 DOZ. 12 LBS.

#2052 COOKY THE CUCUMBER
Tall, trim and terrific is Cooky, and to keep her company is Mr. Potato Head. Set contains plastic cucumber and potato, facial and body parts—over 30 pieces to change these lifelike vegetables into funny, loveable friends. Instructions included. Size 9" x 6" x 3". 2 DOZ. 12 LBS.

#2053 KATIE THE CARROT
Here's one of Mr. Potato Head's very special friends. Together these lifelike vegetables are all ready to be turned into funny, loveable friends. Set contains plastic carrot and potato, facial and body parts. Over 30 pieces total. Instructions included. Size 9" x 6" x 3". 2 DOZ. 12 LBS.

#2054 MR. POTATO HEAD AND HIS TOOTY FROOTY FRIENDS
4 lifelike plastic vegetables in this exciting set. Mr. Potato Head plus 3 of his tooty frooty friends (cucumber, pepper, orange). Set contains over 60 pieces including assorted facial and body parts. Instructions included. Size 13½" x 8" x 3". 1 DOZ. 10 LBS.

#2058 MR. POTATO HEAD AND HIS FRIENDS ASSORTMENT
This special pack features Mr. Potato Head along with all his friends. Included are Pete the Pepper, Oscar the Orange, Cooky the Cucumber, and Katie the Carrot. Packed 6 each to the assortment. Size 9" x 6" x 3". 2 DOZ. 12 LBS.

#2640 TOOTY FROOTY GAME
Fun-filled game is easy to play, easy to assemble. Make a Tooty Frooty friend or even Mr. Potato Head himself. Game contains plastic vegetable heads complete with necessary facial and body parts. Also playing board with plastic spinner. Instructions included. Size 24¾" x 18" x 1¾". 1 DOZ. 23 LBS.

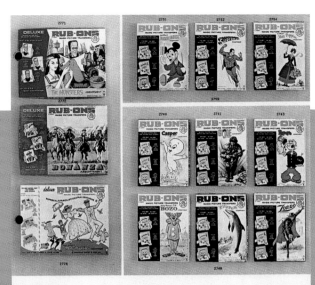

RUB-ONS™... just a rub makes a picture
The most wonderful toy for every girl and boy!

#2778 DELUXE RUB-ONS ASSORTMENT Super size version. Contains: #2771 Munsters, #2772 Bonanza, #2774 Mary Poppins. 16½" x 12¾" x 1¹¹⁄₁₆". 1 Dozen, 14 lbs.

#2759 RUB-ONS ASSORTMENT Contains eight pieces each of #2751 Mickey Mouse, #2752 Superman and #2754 Mary Poppins. 12⅛" x 9¾" x 1". 2 Dozen, 13 lbs.

#2748 RUB-ONS ASSORTMENT Contains four pieces each of #2743 Popeye, #2745 Bozo, #2747 Zorro, #2740 Casper, #2746 Flipper, #2741 G.I. Joe. 12⅛" x 9¾" x 1". 2 Dozen, 13 lbs.

Here's an item with "magic appeal" for children the world over. A coloring toy that will let them make the most beautiful pictures imaginable . . . without paint, crayons or water. All they do is rub on the color from the magic transfer sheet to the outline paper . . . and watch a whole picture come to life in color. It's easy . . . it's fun . . . and there's a wide variety of Rub-Ons you can offer to your customers.

The Regular size Rub-Ons contains three 9" x 11" outline sheets, three 7" x 10" Rub-On sheets and one wooden stylus. Instruction sheet included.

The Super-size Deluxe Rub-Ons contains six 9" x 11" outline sheets, six 7" x 10" Rub-On sheets and one wooden stylus. Instruction sheet included.

Almost all of the cool Batman toys were made this year to coincide with the debut of the TV series. As soon as I saw my neighbor Andy Kenyon running around with his plastic Batman helmet (made by Ideal Toys), I knew I *had* to have one. This was one of my most sacred possessions, as I really felt like the Caped Crusader when I wore it. Amazingly, it still fits me.

The Flying Batman toy was a combination glider and slingshot which never flew as far or as straight as I hoped it would. After several crash landings, I decided there was a reason why Batman never flew in the comics.

The Batman parachute toy was a spinoff of the *Ripcord* parachute man made throughout the '60s. The *Ripcord* figure was an aqua-colored plastic skydiver with a red-and-white-striped plastic chute that you would fold up and then toss skyward. Both the Batman and *Ripcord* parachute toys worked extremely well, and a great thrill for me that summer was dropping Batman out the window of a vacant office building and watching him float down to the sidewalk where pedestrians looked up, amazed. It was terrific fun—until Batman got caught in our walnut tree. By the time our gardener, Frank Sunada, pried him down with the rake, there wasn't much left of him.

During my fun time in the tub, I always enjoyed playing with my Soaky bubble-bath friends like Bozo, Tennessee Tuxedo, and Secret Squirrel. I also enjoyed using the unbreakable clear tube of Prell shampoo as an atomic torpedo—only Batman or Superman could prevent it from destroying all the other Soakys.

I took a lot of flack in kindergarten for showing up with a *Mary Poppins* lunchbox. The class bully, Wynn Wolfe, antagonized me to the point that I almost threw my thermos at him. But I would never sacrifice my chocolate milk to make a point about my masculinity. Next up for me was the more unisex *Peanuts* lunchbox, which I loved because of the Christmas and Halloween TV specials in which the characters starred.

Lisa Klein, our neighbor and a runner-up favorite babysitter of mine, had this "Go Go" thermos and a matching patent-leather bag. She was the type of girl you would see dancing barefoot to the radio in cutoff Levis. In 1966, she was the neighborhood "It" Girl, complete with her purple Slik Chik Sting-Ray.

This extremely rare Shrimpenstein doll was sold in stores in late '66 to take advantage of the popularity of the local TV show.

Although the classic-monster craze had peaked before '66, I still loved these plastic monster figures (made by Marx) of the Wolf Man, Frankenstein, the Hunchback, Phantom of the Opera, the Creature from the Black Lagoon, and the Mummy. I watched the classic Universal horror films on local TV and looked at pictures of them in *Famous Monsters* magazine.

The Marvel superheroes appeared as Marx figures as their syndicated cartoon show granted them new popularity.

Secret Agent Halloween costume: This extremely sophisticated knockoff of the Green Hornet suit enabled me to be either the Hornet or John Drake, the star of my favorite TV spy show, *Secret Agent*. This costume was the perfect complement to my Secret Sam attaché case.

If I were to think about the one characteristic that most distinguished all my playthings from 1966, it would be *imagination*. These most prized possessions of my young years featured fantasy elements and many different characters, and this imaginative diversity would help me to develop my creative skills, my curiosity, and my sense of wonderment about the world. In addition, they made me appreciate my parents, who paid for all this stuff!

Why did the little boy throw the
clock out the window?

He wanted to see time fly.

5 READING

One of the most remarkable things about being a kid in 1966 was that you didn't need a lot of technology to bring an incredible visual world right into your bedroom. There were no computers or high-tech video games, so, other than television and radio, the easiest way to escape the pressures of grammar school was to pick up a book, a magazine, or a comic book.

I fondly remember purchasing many of these wondrous books and periodicals at the local family-owned market in my neighborhood, which was called Bestway. It was a real "general store" like the one Sam Drucker ran on *Petticoat Junction*—complete with a post office in the back. While my mom shopped, I always gazed at the comic book rack and the paperback books. In the later '60s, I remember slipping the *Playboy*s inside of *Look* magazines. I think I got caught because the storeowner wondered why a kid would be interested in *Look* magazine.

Like so much of the decade, the year 1966 was filled with kaleidoscopic, imaginative images for me, which came through the pages of many of my favorite reading materials.

Green Lantern was my favorite DC Comics superhero. It had to be his ultra-cool stylish costume: Green Hornet–type emerald mask, white gloves, and no cape to hassle with! Plus his name was appealing to me—Hal Jordan.

This was my very first Batman comic. It was given to me by my neighbor Sparky Rifkin, who collected DC Comics in neat, orderly piles separated by character. The villain in this story seemed to be wearing my very first Halloween costume, the ubiquitous "skeleton suit."

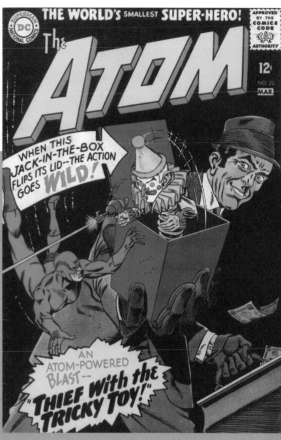

The second DC Comic that Sparky gave me had a romantic theme: Lois decides between waiting for Superman and marrying Lance Fortune. (I would have thought Bruce Wayne.) I was relieved when Lance turned out to be Superman in disguise.

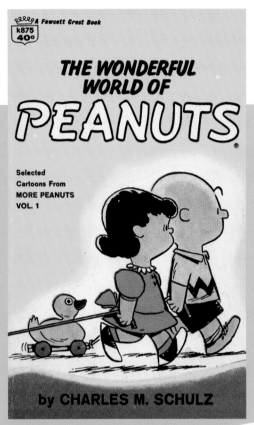

I loved reading this Bozo storybook, in which Bozo and Butchy Boy befriend a runaway ape from the circus.

The children's magazine *Jack and Jill* was the first periodical to which my parents bought me a subscription.

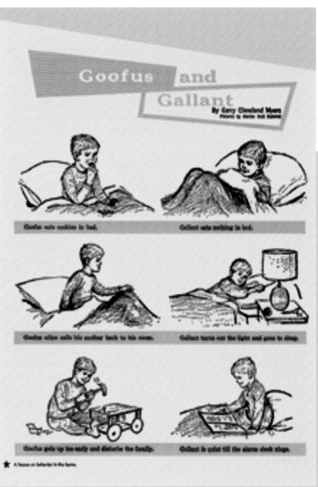

Highlights . . . I always loved the "Hidden Pictures" and the diametrically opposed antics of "Goofus and Gallant." I always related more to Goofus, who reminded me of Dennis the Menace.

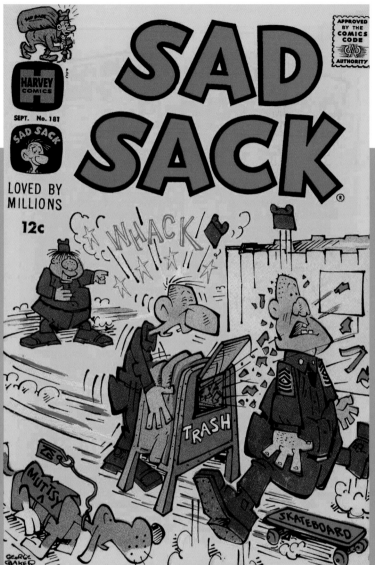

Sad Sack and the spin-off comic *Gabby Gob* (a navy version of *Sad Sack*) were real faves. I didn't really begin to relate to the army-barracks premise of *Sad Sack* until I started watching *Gomer Pyle* on TV, but Sad Sack's bumbling underdog persona reminded me of Gilligan, and the burly, grouchy Sarge was a clone of the Skipper (although *Sad Sack* predates *Gilligan's Island* by several years).

Other Harvey Comics characters I enjoyed reading about while lying atop my twin bed in my pajamas emblazoned with gas station signs included Richie Rich, Little Audrey, Hot Stuff, Little Lotta, Little Dot, Stumbo the Giant, and Casper the Friendly Ghost. (I was never crazy about Casper—he seemed a little too wimpy. I preferred his tough-guy buddy Spooky, sort of the Goofus of the ghost world.)

Above is a rare spin-off title of the Sad Sack series . . . *Little Sad Sack*—an attempt to ride the wave of the immense popularity of the *Peanuts* comics. The biggest-selling *Peanuts* paperback of '66 was unquestionably *Snoopy and the Red Baron*. Later this year, the band the Royal Guardsmen immortalized Snoopy's struggle in the pop hit "Snoopy vs. the Red Baron."

While several of these were first published in the 1950s, I read them every holiday season as a kid, including in 1966. I remember piling into my parents' '63 powder blue Ford Country Squire wagon to visit Candy Cane Lane, a wonderfully charming spectacle of lights and lawn decorations that still appears every December to this day in the San Fernando Valley. These books made the holiday season extremely special for me, as did the incredible TV specials like *A Charlie Brown Christmas* ('65) and *How the Grinch Stole Christmas*, which premiered in '66. While reading these magical books I would have some mini candy canes, a chocolate marshmallow Santa, and a glass of eggnog served in one of my family's red and green "Tom and Jerry" eggnog mugs. Even today, when I drink my eggnog during the holiday season, I think of these vivid memories of Santa Claus and how excited I was when my mom took me to greet him at the local mall.

I was exposed to many outstanding depictions of teen culture in 1966. I especially enjoyed reading about Archie and his pals—their lifestyle and day-to-day activities in mythical Riverdale, U.S.A., were so easy to relate to.

Even *Archie* cashed in on the superhero craze of '66.

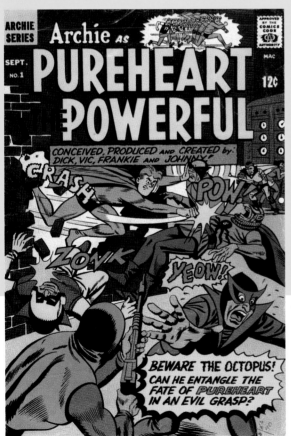

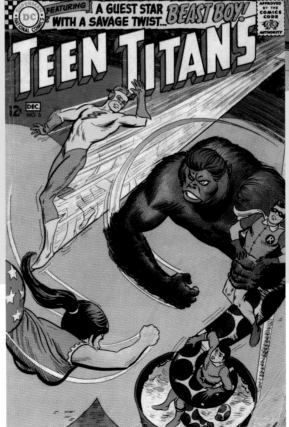

DC Comics cornered the youth market with the super-cool and extremely agile *Teen Titans* featuring Robin the Boy Wonder, Kid Flash, Aqualad, and Wonder Girl, the first superheroes to carry transistor radios.

In 1966, DC Comics also created a series of teen-inspired titles similar to *Archie*. They started with *Swing with Scooter*, which incorporated mod, Carnaby Street fashions, vespa scooters, and rock music in a very unique hybrid comic that taught me a lot about a lifestyle that would not be my own until the early '70s.

Also in 1966, comedian Bob Hope became the guardian of a wild bunch of teens at Benedict Arnold High School, where monsters and ghouls were depicted alongside students, and there was even a superhero named "Super-Hip" who played rock guitar à la Conrad Birdie in *Bye Bye Birdie*. This particular comic is one of the rarest and most collectible of the '60s. I first discovered it during a family trip to Palm Springs, where I picked up a copy at a Thrifty drugstore (along with a box of Red Hots) and immediately fell for the zany premise and colorful imagery.

Finally, the last undeniably hip teen comic of '66 came in the form of a campy, offbeat, and extremely clever update of the classic '40s comics starring Plastic Man, created by Jack Cole.

CLASSIC TEEN MAGS

These magazines taught me about the world that teenagers in my neighborhood were experiencing. I envied those lucky few who got to see the Beatles perform at Dodger Stadium that year. I would converse with our babysitters about the stories featured in these publications and, while eating Jiffy Pop, would hear all the latest gossip from these Gidget types on Herman's Hermits, the Rolling Stones, Chad and Jeremy, Nancy Sinatra, and, of course, the Fab Four, whose big single in the summer of '66 was "Paperback Writer."

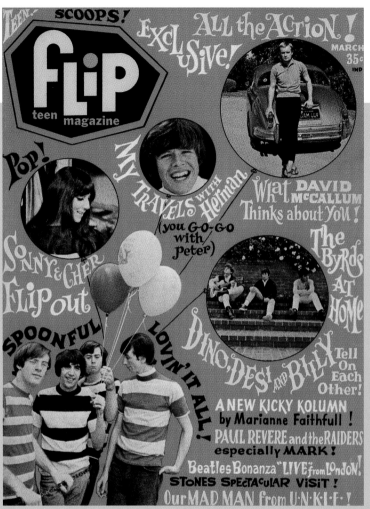

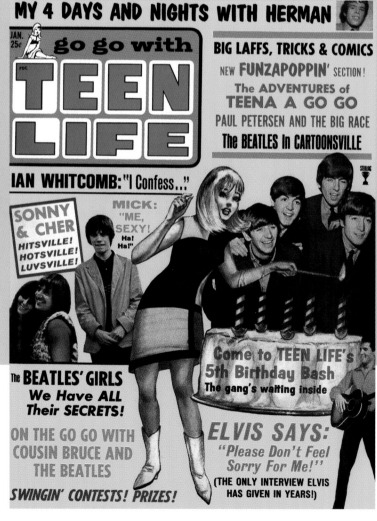

BEATLES EXPLODE!

OCT/25¢

"THOSE NASTY LIES WE HATE!"
50 FREAKIE NEW PIX
"THEIR SECRET LIVES" BY NEIL

16 MAGAZINE

FANG: *"COME HOME WITH ME—MEET MY FOLKS!"*

MARK: *"THE LONELY YEARS I CAN'T FORGET"*

SMITTY: *"COLOR ME BLUE & PINK & KISS ME!"*

HERMAN & HERMITS WILL BE YOUR PEN-PAL & SEND YOU GIFTS!

DC5 BEATLES RAIDERS PAUL McC. KEITH A. | **WILDEST NEW COLOR PIN-UPS**

McCALLUM – VAUGHN WHAT ARE THEY HIDING?

FREE HUGE TOP STAR COLOR SCRAPBOOK
STONES ★ B-BOYS
THOMAS GROUP ★ TIMMY ROONEY

HOLLYWOOD GOGO TEEN ALBUM

35¢ No. 8

WOW! Your Own **BATMAN & ROBIN SCRAPBOOK!**

plus: **GIANT CONTEST—CREATE A NEW VILLAIN** for B&R!

SOCK! Your Favorite Comic Strip Characters Come To Life!

HOW TO BE AN ELVIS GIRL
Special Scorecard Inside

CONTEST BONANZA

WIN THE SHIRT OFF HERMAN'S BACK
WIN A PHONE CALL FROM CHRIS CONNELLY
WIN A HULLABALOO GO GO WARDROBE

THE SPIES STRIP FOR *ACTION!*
McCallum · Connery · Coburn

CATCH THAT GUY AND KEEP HIM— SALLY SHOWS YOU HOW!

DATE-TIME DIRECTORY: 60 DREAMY BACHELORS

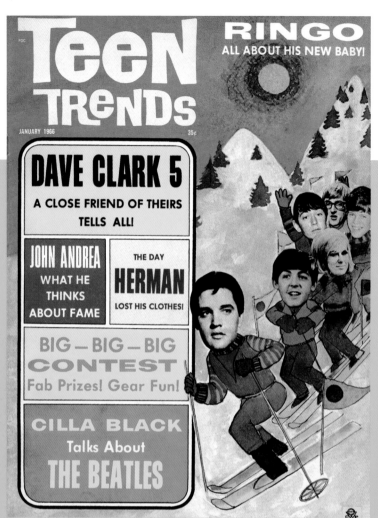

It seemed that teen culture permeated so much of the media in 1966. It was the overriding social theme of the decade. Television shows, fashion, and music were all targeted to the youth market, and it was the first time in modern history that adults really took on the same interests as their children.

One magazine that brilliantly combined adult satire with comic book culture was *MAD* magazine. It was first published in the '50s, but really took hold of '60s pop culture in a very sophisticated manner. *MAD* was the first "adult" magazine I ever really read and kind of understood even as a preteen. The movie and TV parodies were razor-sharp and the artwork was ingenious.

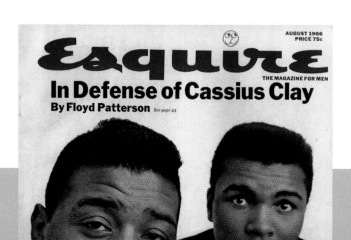

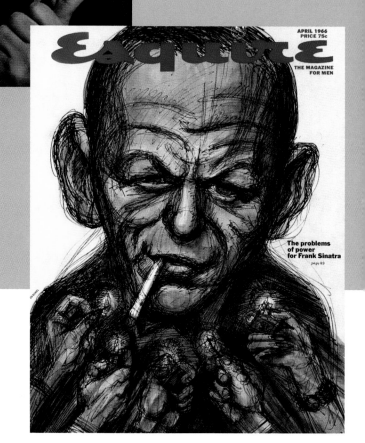

Moving on into the adult world of reading material, there was *Esquire* magazine, which was very literary and upscale. I wasn't reading this kind of material yet, but I remember seeing copies on my parents' black-and-white marble coffee table.

This cover story, "Frank Sinatra Has a Cold" by Gay Talese, is one of the finest, most compelling portraits of Frank Sinatra ever written. The title refers to the complete anxiety Sinatra would experience when his voice was even a little scratchy. I didn't read this article until many years later, but I consider it a major journalistic triumph of 1966.

Playboy magazine was very hip and trendy in this year. Just over a decade old, *Playboy* really hit its stride in the mid '60s and covered all facets of pop culture for guys in college and beyond. Throughout the '60s, *Playboy* featured some of the most clever cover photography I have ever seen in a magazine, and '66 was certainly no exception. Ads for Brylcreem, sports cars, stereos, and sporting equipment all embodied the spirit of the "What kind of man reads *Playboy*?" ads that ran in each issue.

Hugh Hefner described *Playboy* as "an urban handbook" that beautified, not objectified, women. At age six, since my reading skills were somewhat limited, I could only look at Playboy for the pictures, not the articles, which may have had a progressive influence on my character. . . . I was the only kid in first grade wearing Hai Karate cologne and a gold ascot.

My father, who worked in the wholesale liquor industry, would get complimentary copies of *Playboy* sent to him because of the liquor ads it contained. So occasionally I would see these tucked away in his nightstand (of course, even Dad had the good sense to conceal them inside of *Look* magazines).

LOOK

35 CENTS · OCTOBER 4, 1966

ABOARD A FLYING SAUCER
The incredible story of two people who believe they were "kidnapped" by humanoids in a spacecraft

ELIZABETH TAYLOR
Does Burton tame the shrew as Shakespeare intended?

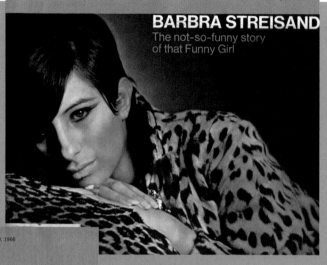

LOOK

35 CENTS · APRIL 5, 1966

GENERAL RIDGWAY
condemns "all-out war" in Vietnam

CATHOLIC EDUCATION'S TIME BOMB
The crisis that led to revolt at St. John's University could overturn the entire system

BARBRA STREISAND
The not-so-funny story of that Funny Girl

LOOK

35 CENTS · SEPTEMBER 20, 1966

THE OPEN GENERATION

Their new morality
Conversations parents never hear
Early sex and early marriage
London's cutting edge
Russia's cool Communists

YOUTH '66

In '66, *Look* magazine featured some of the most powerful women in show business and politics. Elizabeth Taylor starred in the film *Who's Afraid of Virginia Woolf?* Barbra Streisand was fresh off the success of *Funny Girl* on Broadway. Jackie Kennedy was rebuilding her stature as an American icon.

LOOK

35 CENTS · MARCH 22, 1966

OUR HOSPITALS ARE KILLING US

An alarming report on conditions in many American cities

SCHOOL TESTS

Do they help learning or invite cheating?

JACQUELINE KENNEDY TODAY

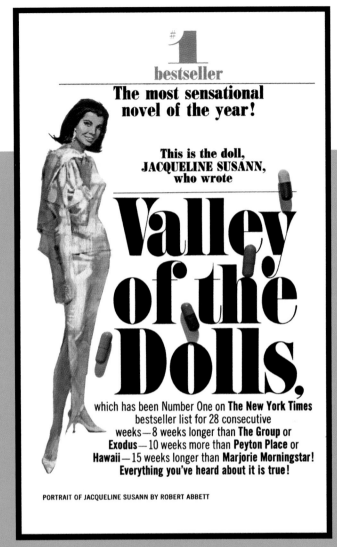

#1 bestseller
The most sensational novel of the year!

This is the doll, JACQUELINE SUSANN, who wrote

Valley of the Dolls,

which has been Number One on **The New York Times** bestseller list for 28 consecutive weeks—8 weeks longer than **The Group** or **Exodus**—10 weeks more than **Peyton Place** or **Hawaii**—15 weeks longer than **Marjorie Morningstar!** **Everything you've heard about it is true!**

PORTRAIT OF JACQUELINE SUSANN BY ROBERT ABBETT

R1082 60¢   A Fawcett Crest Book

PHYLLIS DILLER'S housekeeping hints

"Cleaning your house while your kids are still growing, is like shoveling the walk before it stops showing"

Introduction by
Bob Hope

Over on my mom's nightstand was the best-selling paperback novel of the year and the decade, Jacqueline Susann's *Valley of the Dolls*, a steamy, controversial, tragic tale of desire and decadence in the darkest corners of show business. (I always thought it was about the valley I lived in—the San Fernando Valley!) I also remember seeing on my mom's nightstand *Phyllis Diller's Housekeeping Hints*, which may have explained why none of my socks ever matched and why the peanut butter and jelly were always on the outside of my sandwiches!

"But that's not the way we do it in school, Mother!"

This simple statement underlines your child's growing need for The World Book Encyclopedia at home.

...selling encyclopedia ...volumes contain over —and over 1,900 maps. ...wn, $6 a month available.

The most advantageous thing about all of the reading I did in 1966 is that it really prepared me for all the years of schoolwork that lay ahead. I developed very solid study habits—and learned some of the shortcuts, too.

KING LEAR NOTES

Cliffs Notes

DON'T WaiT TiLL COLLEGE

6 FASHION

Fashion designs of 1966 were extremely progressive, creative, and visually appealing. The British music invasion of '64 was still influencing pop culture, so fashion styles from London, Paris, and Italy continued to dominate fashion trends around the world. Here in the U.S., women's clothing took on even more bold and exciting colors and patterns. Wild paisleys, bright citrus colors, and sexually aggressive hemlines predominated.

In 1966, men's fashions become more feminine looking: slim pants, multi-patterned prints, and an androgynous overall look made for an interesting twist in the sexual revolution of the '60s. Men still wanted to appear masculine, but, just like women, they also wanted to look psychedelic and "tuned-in" to the counterculture.

I remember that in this year my father purchased his first bottle of Hai Karate after-shave as well as the other exotic, tiki-culture cologne called Jade East (which was commonly featured in *Playboy* in '66, along with Brut by Faberge). I remember making quite a splash with my first-grade female colleagues when I arrived to class doused in Hai Karate, smelling sexy and dangerous. It was quite a sight to see them karate-chopping their desks in half to try and sit closer to the one man in the classroom who exuded both innocence and mystery.

One of the most popular fragrances for men in 1966 was a twist of lime. Maybe this was to give guys the subtle aroma of a cocktail. . . .

for men...

exhilarating elegance...

JADE EAST®

COLOGNE AND AFTER SHAVE

COLOGNE $4.50 AFTER SHAVE $3.50   SWANK, NEW YORK – SOLE DISTRIBUTOR

HIM FEEL INTERESTING. AVON FOR MEN HAS VARIETY, CONVENIENCE, AND STYLE. ONLY YOUR AVON REPRESENTATIVE CAN SHOW YOU THESE DISTINCTIVE TOILETRIES.

AVON CALLING has many ways to help a man look great!

AVON FOR MEN

©1966 Avon Products., Inc.

LOOK 4-19-66 95

Dress by Estevez

Get that "we're-off-in-the-Ferrari" feeling in the Forward Fashion Look. There's thrust in the shoulder, power in the lean line, sparkle in the color. Life is more exciting every day you wear it. Tailored with the dedicated Daroff Personal Touch, it has that Tapered-Trim slim, athletic design. You'll come on strong, shift your life into go, help things happen when you put a little Forward Fashion in your life. Suit pictured is Pongee Weave at $79.95. Other lightweight suits in Darolite, Daroglo and Daro-Poplon, $69.95 to $75.00. Sport Coats, $42.95 to $65.00. Slacks, $17.95 to $29.95. America's No. 1 Quality-Value.

'BOTANY' 500 *TAILORED BY DAROFF*

Featuring exclusive blends of DACRON* polyester and worsted. For free fashion booklet and name of dealer, write: H. Daroff & Sons, Inc., 2300 Walnut Street, Phila. 3, Pa. (a subsidiary of Botany Industries). Prices slightly higher in the West. Linings Sanitized® treated for hygienic freshness. Also available in Canada, Peru and Australia.

My dad's fashion taste in '66 was far more conservative than the "hip generation"; he favored streamlined Botany 500 suits, not unlike the style Dick Van Dyke wore on his TV show.

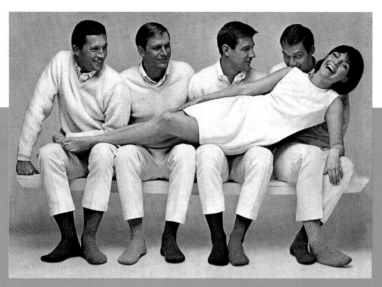

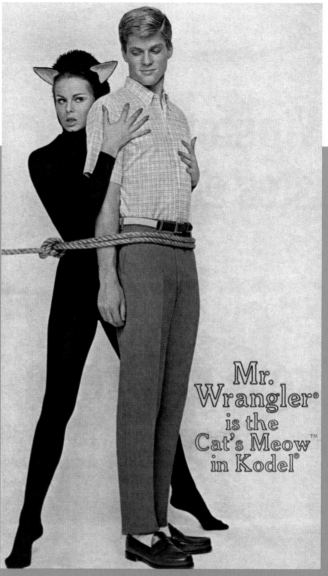

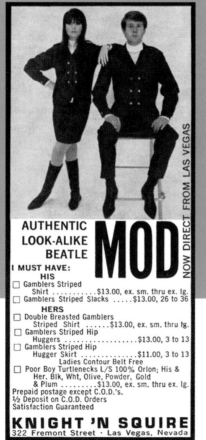

In '66, most of the teenagers and college-aged guys in my neighborhood were still wearing the earlier '60s collegiate look, which was in sharp contrast to the overt, sexually aggressive look that women favored during this transitional year in fashion.

Men were still wearing the Beatle boots that had come into vogue in 1964. Women were wearing all different kinds of boots—which of course was fueled by the smashing success of Nancy Sinatra's "These Boots Are Made for Walkin'" in January of this year.

Nancy Sinatra had an obvious influence on this '66 issue of *Millie the Model.*

BIRDS OF A HEATHER
SWING TOGETHER!

How do you make a bird-watcher watch you?
to the mating-call of the singingest, swingingest chic's
scene! Choose from a Christmas Tree-Q of colors...

VOGUE

75¢
MAY

THIS
SUMMER'S
FASHION
75 WONDERFUL
NEW WAYS
TO LOOK

THIS
SUMMER'S
BEAUTY:
THE NEW
SKIN IDEA

Mia Farrow—breakaway

The Carnaby Street mod look was in full force in 1966, and designers like Mary Quant (famous for the miniskirt) and Rudi Gernreich (famous for "cut-out" clothing) were all the rage. Gernreich was one of the most influential designers of the twentieth century, and he played a very significant role in 1966 pop culture. (He even guest-starred with Catwoman in an episode of *Batman*.) He also invented the transparent and wireless "no bra" bra.

Twiggy became the most successful and influential "It" Girl of 1966. Famous for her Q-tip figure and Peter Pan haircut, Twiggy was a major influence on 1966 fashion. She motivated Mia Farrow to change her look dramatically.

for the lively ones

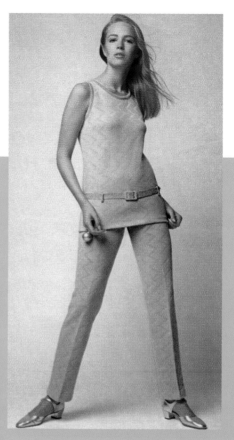

Monochromatic looks on
women were very popular in
this year and the next. I fondly
remember my second-grade
teacher, Miss Schorr, wearing
these single-color outfits—in my
imagination, she resembled a
human Crayola.

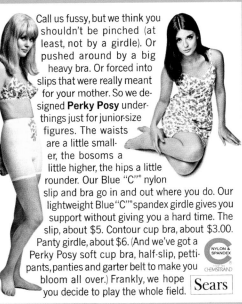

I vividly remember going with my parents to Bullocks department store at the Fashion Square Mall, and to Sears where we would always get incredible popcorn and chocolate raisins. My brother and I sneaked off to the teenage girls department one time and took in some sights that propelled us immediately forward into manhood. This was like a behind-the-scenes tour of Gidget's closet. I couldn't wait to turn 10!

TEEN • Young America's Fashion, Beauty & Entertainment Magazine

'TEEN

MARCH 1966 35c

special
custom body issue

Total your figure
Shape up for fun
Fashion your frame

THE STRANGE MALE STRANGER

SWINGING OFFSPRING
Dino, Desi and Billy
Board Chairman, Jr.

STRAIGHT FROM CALIFORNIA
Hang Ten Hair

'TEEN gives you a new slant...

...on beauty, fashion, fads, fiction

'TEEN • Young America's Fashion, Beauty & Entertainment Magazine

'TEEN

JUNE 1966 35c

GIANT SURFARI ISSUE

57 WILD WILD SWIM SUITS

THE BEACH BOYS THE TURTLES

BEAUTY WAYVES
primitive blondes
bronzed bods

HOW TO SURF *ANYWHERE*

HOW TO BE A BEACH BUM

Teen magazine was the first choice of most of my babysitters during this year, and leafing through some of these issues helped me understand the opposite sex a little better. I started dressing a little snazzier myself as I began my James Bond fashion phase.

Pre-supermodel Cheryl Tiegs on the June issue of *Teen* magazine.

In the summer of '66, fueled by the Beach Boys' masterpiece single "Good Vibrations," California beach culture took a turn towards more exotic and daring bathing suit designs. I remember spotting teenage girls dancing in the sand at Sorrento Beach in Santa Monica to a transistor radio blasting "96 Tears" by Question Mark and the Mysterians. It was a watershed moment in my young life that I never forgot. I remember drinking ice-cold Orange Crush out of the bottle and eating my mom's egg salad sandwiches on Roman Meal bread. Ironically, in this year the classic "beach party" films of '63 through '65 were beginning to wind down as women's lib and progressive social leaders like Betty Friedan were creating a stronger, more independent image for women around the world. I felt this transition as my favorite babysitter, Debbie Gibson, moved away to go to college, leaving the sands of Santa Monica for the hallowed halls of UCLA.

VOGUE

75¢
APR.1

QUICK
PREVIEW
OF
SUMMER
FASHION

THE
BEAUTIFUL
PEOPLE:
SUMMER
LOOKS
THEY
LOVE

BEAUTY
TIPS
FROM SAVVY
TRAVELLERS

LIFE

Jonathan Daniels
writes more about

F.D.R.'s
Secret
Romance

'I do not
feel I have
peeped
and told'

First color pictures

FALL
FASHIONS
FROM PARIS—
THE
LIVELIEST
EVER

St. Laurent's
pop-art version
of how to dress
for dinner

SEPTEMBER 2 · 1966 · 50¢

Sophisticated ladies in '66 wore
designers such as Andre Courreges,
Emilio Pucci, and Pierre Cardin. Here
Raquel Welch steps out in style.

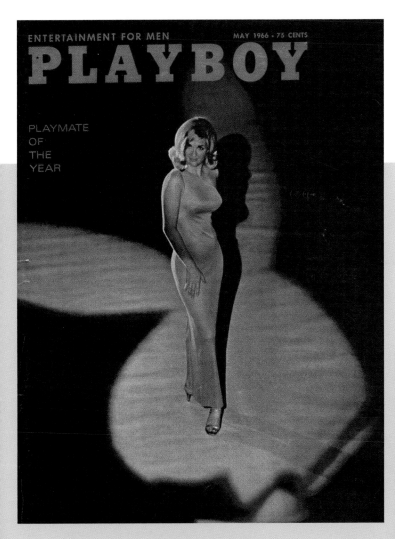

Most of my exposure to women's
eveningwear came when my mom
would get dressed up for a fancy dinner
with my dad at the Sportsmen's Lodge
or Trader Vic's. The only other time this
year that I got to see women's dress-up
clothes was during prom season, when
pink satin gowns and long white gloves
seemed to flood the neighborhood.

Stripes, Spots and Tina Louise

Better plan on stalking wild animals this season. Jungle fever is spreading across the country. Animal fashions—fake or real—are what we are talking about. And wouldn't the boys like to go on safari with gorgeous Tina Louise of Gilligan's Island? Above: Double-breasted cheetah coat is from Somaliland. $1900. From Fuhrman's Furs, Beverly Hills.

Wild-animal prints were extremely popular, and they exemplified the predatory nature of the '66 fashion attitude. In 1966, women got tougher and more self-assured. Their fashion sense had a "shoot to kill" attitude about it that created a platform on which the women's movement could be founded. (The leopard print look made a strong comeback beginning in the 1990s, with the rise in popularity of lounge music and martini bars.)

Lots of synthetic clothing materials were popular in 1966. They boasted wrinkle-free qualities but were probably just less expensive than more natural fabrics. Many of the synthetic fabrics were trademarked: Kodel polyester, Banlon nylon, Dacron polyester/cotton, and Arnel triacetate. Models such as Jean Shrimpton, Marissa Berenson, Peggy Moffit, and, of course, Twiggy, wore all of these materials with overwhelming visual allure and splendor.

Beeline's fall '66 fashion showings start right now.

Penneys
ALWAYS FIRST QUALITY

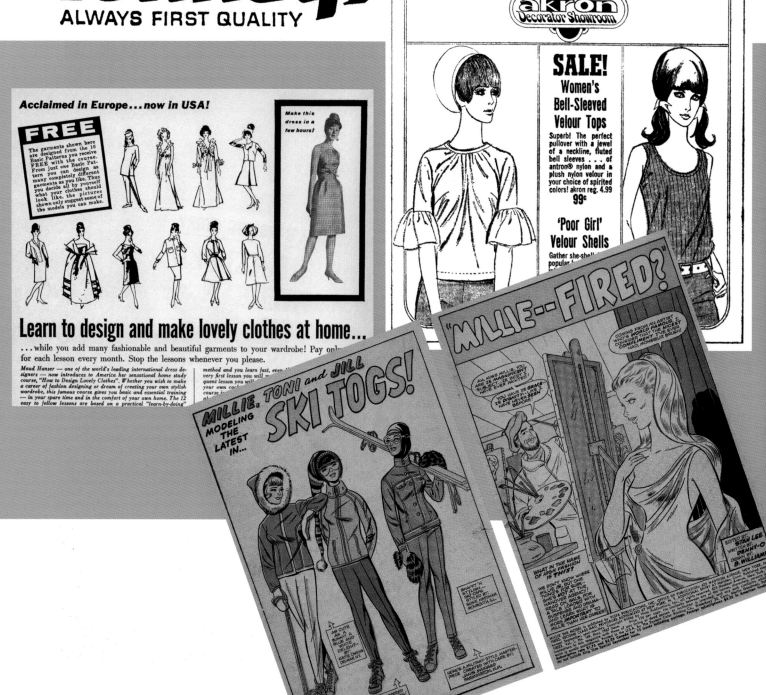

lip gloss
makes the scene

get the slick and shiny mouth that's shaking up the fashion scene. whip lip gloss over or under your lipstick. keeps lips smooth, soft and inviting in all seasons. isn't that what it's all about?

**Lip Gloss
by Max Factor**

© 1966, MAX FACTOR & CO. AVAILABLE IN CANADA.

Lip Lip Hooray!

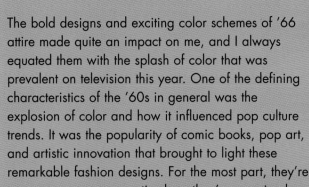

For one-two-three-four lipcolors by Max Factor that mix-and-match or glow it alone.

For a happy new brush that swishes on color, then swivels into a disappearing act.

For a whole crazy wardrobe of brush-on lipcolors that Max Factor has just put into a chic little mirrored case. For who? You!

Lip Lip Hooray!
a palette of lipcolors
by Max Factor

The bold designs and exciting color schemes of '66 attire made quite an impact on me, and I always equated them with the splash of color that was prevalent on television this year. One of the defining characteristics of the '60s in general was the explosion of color and how it influenced pop culture trends. It was the popularity of comic books, pop art, and artistic innovation that brought to light these remarkable fashion designs. For the most part, they're timeless; they've remained contemporary throughout the twentieth and, now, twenty-first centuries. There is no doubt in my mind that '60s fashion, in particular the fashion of 1966 and 1967, will live forever in our minds—and on the racks of the world's finest boutiques and department stores.

*Max Factor creates the sheer miracle
of UltraLucent Pressed Powder*

A finish so nearly nude it could be nothing at all, and yet so perfectly blended that flaws, tiny lines and imperfections seem to disappear.

Ultra-light, ultra-smooth, ultra-sheer... a radiantly soft transparency that looks like nature's own. A full range of natural skin tones captured in new UltraLucent Pressed Powder... from The Luxurious UltraLucent Collection
by **Max Factor**

How comfortable can sun glasses be? You'll never know until you slip on a pair of Ray-Bans, the quality sun glass. Lenses of real optical glass scientifically block harmful rays. Reduce glare to cool, soft light. You'll like the way they fit and feel on your face, too. Solid. Not loose or flimsy. And they come in more styles than you can shake a fashion designer at. You have to go to one of the better stores to buy them. But they're worth the trip. Available in your prescription, too. Write for free style folder. Smart Ray-Ban Sun Glasses by Bausch & Lomb, Rochester, New York 14602.

BAUSCH & LOMB
Ray-Ban
the most distinguished name in SUN GLASSES

Marché   *Olympian III*   *Pasha C*

7 FOOD&DRINK

One of the principal advantages of being six years old in 1966 was that I didn't have to worry about calorie intake or cholesterol levels, but instead could choose from a wide variety of culinary delights. This chapter highlights the many innovative and delectable foods and beverages I enjoyed. Be forewarned: after reading it, you may be tempted to tear into a box of Good and Plenty or drink a nice "Fruit Juicy" Hawaiian Punch.

What I remember best about the foods of '66 was the creative and colorful packaging. So many of my favorite products and restaurants also featured entertaining mascot characters—Lucky the Leprechaun, Cap'n Crunch, Jack the Clown (from Jack in the Box). As a kid, I saw them not as product spokesmen, but as legitimate cartoon stars in the same league as Underdog and Bugs Bunny.

Every morning at the breakfast table, I would normally feast on a huge bowl of one of my favorite cereals. In 1966, my top-of-the-line choices were: Cap'n Crunch, Twinkles, Froot Loops, or Lucky Charms.

In 1963, the *Rocky and Bullwinkle* team at Jay Ward Productions produced the first commercials for Cap'n Crunch cereal. Daws Butler (voice of Yogi Bear, Huckleberry Hound, and tons of other cartoon characters) provided the voice of the foggy Cap'n. Various additional flavors of the cereal started appearing in the later '60s, beginning with "Crunch Berries." The Ward studios also produced commercials for Quisp and Quake cereals, which first appeared in late '66. Both of these cereals, although shaped differently, tasted very much like Cap'n Crunch. (Quisp made an auspicious comeback to supermarket shelves in the late '90s.)

Twinkles was a truly magical breakfast cereal from General Mills. Its trademark feature in the earlier '60s was that an actual comic book appeared on the back of the box, featuring the mascot character, Twinkles the elephant. In '66, the box design changed and the cereal became the star. During the mid '60s, Rocky and Bullwinkle pitched several of the General Mills cereals in TV commercials, most notably Cheerios. Dudley Do-Right later appeared on the Frosty O's box from General Mills.

Sixty-six Froot Loops box featuring Toucan Sam and an offer for a Batman periscope. This box always reminded me of many happy visits to the Enchanted Tiki Room at Disneyland, which has remained pretty much the same for the past forty years. Trix was my other favorite fruit-flavored cereal in '66—I thought it *must* be healthier than Cocoa Puffs.

Sixty-six version of "magically delicious" Lucky Charms. How I used to love plucking out the marshmallows—especially the yellow moons, which I always imagined to be banana-flavored. Coincidentally, in the mid '60s General Mills produced a short-lived but delightful cereal called Banana Wackies. It was an oat mix similar to Lucky Charms, but it featured banana-flavored marshmallows.

NEW CHIFFON MARGARINE

Chiffon Margarine

net wt. 1 lb.

Chiffon Margarine

SO SOFT...IT COMES IN A TUB

My parents always favored "serious" breakfast cereals like Shredded Wheat, and tried to feed me English muffins with Chiffon margarine to make sure I ate a balanced diet. To start my morning right, I would add a tall glass of Tang, which supposedly provided me with a full day's supply of vitamin C. In retrospect, it was more like tangerine Kool-Aid. When we ran out of Tang, I would sometimes try to replicate the taste by dropping a few orange-flavored Johnson's Baby Aspirins in a glass of water . . . definitely not the same as Fizzies. (Fizzies, for those of you who may not remember, were powdered drink tablets that dissolved like Alka-Seltzer. You would drop one in a glass and it would fizz and foam into a Kool-Aid–type beverage . . . very "Secret Agent Man.")

Start off your team with more vitamin C.

Start off your team with Tang. The NFL does. Tang is the official breakfast drink on every National Football League training table. How come? Tang has more vitamin C than any orange juice you can buy. More vitamin A, too. With natural orange flavor. Latch on to a good thing. Kick off your family's day with Tang.

GF GENERAL FOODS KITCHENS

Tang is a trademark of the General Foods Corp.

Sambo's RESTAURANTS

The Fun Place For Family Food

Back in '66 I enjoyed a lot of simple and nourishing lunch and dinnertime foods. Many of these Mom would have to prepare, because they required the stove and, at this stage of the game, I wasn't even allowed to use my Creepy Crawlers "Thingmaker" oven without adult supervision.

One of my favorite lunches was always the golden-brown corn dogs and fresh-squeezed lemonade from Hot Dog on a Stick. The original location at Muscle Beach opened in 1946 and is still in business today. For lunch at home, Chef Boyardee was the king of our kitchen. His spaghetti and meatballs might not have been authentic Italian, but Mom would spice up the presentation with a red and white checked tablecloth and a Chianti bottle filled with Welch's grape juice.

Campbell's vegetable soup was always a staple, but my favorite was the more "gourmet" Andersen's split pea soup, which is still sold in cans today. I loved eating at Bob's Big Boy because they had triple-thick milkshakes and outstanding chili that, for a while, was sold in the frozen-foods section of the grocery store. Also notable from Bob's was their blue cheese dressing, which to this day is still an awesome delight. When eating at home, we'd frequently have Hormel chili, which wasn't as good as Bob's but got the job done. Another favorite dinner for my dad and me was the frozen chicken pie that we always had with an iceberg lettuce salad and Kraft French dressing (which I always loved because of its bright orange color).

Let me help you keep in shape for 1966!

Low Calorie

Low Calorie
KRAFT
French Style
DRESSING

You always eat better with Campbell's

Campbell's
CONDENSED
TOMATO
SOUP

Hormel Chili

Where's the fire?

When your little brigade comes a-runnin', you'll know you've rung the bell with Banquet Chicken Pies. Tender chicken, peas and pimientos, creamy sauce, flaky crust. Expensive? No, chief! Just *tastes* expensive!

thank g♥♥dness for
Banquet
frozen foods

Banquet chicken pie

"it's finger lickin' good"®

A real treat would be venturing out to the Jack in the Box drive-thru, where my brother and I would elbow each other to get to the car window and shout our orders at Jack the Clown. I always preferred Jack in the Box to McDonald's because of the circus-like visual presentation and the local TV show tie-in *Jack in the Box*, which ran on KHJ Channel 9 in L.A. in '66. (The show was hosted by Jack and Phyllis Spear, who in the earlier '60s had starred in *Pip the Piper*.) The Jack in the Box restaurants were the first I remember to use a minimalist "pop art" motif in their architectural design and labeling—all the wrappers and cups simply said "Jack Cola," "Taco," "Moby Jack" for the fish sandwich, and "Bonus Jack" for their big deluxe burger.

I was somewhat discouraged in the late '60s when Ralston Purina bought out Jack in the Box, because I just couldn't fathom that the company that made my favorite tacos also made cat food. They even printed Purina's red-and-white-check logo on their wrappers for a while . . . *not* a strong visual selling point.

My family also enjoyed a big bucket of Kentucky Fried Chicken on the weekends, and I savored their mashed potatoes and gravy. I remember the "No Lie, Free Pie" ad campaign, which featured a cherry pie giveaway in honor of Washington's Birthday. They followed it up with "No Joke, Free Coke," which didn't tantalize me as much . . . I was an Orange Crush and root beer man. In the '60s there were five great root beers: Frostie (with the little elf on the bottle), Hires, Dad's, A & W, and Shasta (loved the commercials with the people blowing the heads of foam off at each other!). Kentucky Fried Chicken also made it to a lot of family picnics. Since I'm a drummer, you can guess what my favorite piece was.

Shakey's Pizza Parlor was a terrific place to dine with the family, or with the team after a Little League game. I always wanted a pitcher of root beer all to myself, and I still remember watching silent movies at Shakey's (and Straw Hat Pizza) starring Laurel and Hardy and Charlie Chaplin. I never understood the significance of the sawdust on the restaurant floor, unless it meant they didn't have to sweep it as much. In the latter part of the year, a Farrell's Ice Cream Parlor opened in the Valley; it utilized much the same turn-of-the-century motif as Shakey's. Farrell's most famous ice cream dish was "the Zoo," a Matterhorn of ice cream and toppings. When it came time to deliver the Zoo to your table, a siren would blare, and several waiters would run through the place carrying your order on a stretcher. This was the highlight of my Cub Scout experience—going to Shakey's and Farrell's.

When all else failed, Mom could always pop in a Swanson's TV dinner. My favorite was definitely the turkey . . . it was like a mini Thanksgiving feast, but I never really trusted the stuffing.

Everybody's
Bugling!

In 1853

a chef in Saratoga Springs, New York
accidentally cooked up a new snack...
potato chips!

In 1966

General Mills brings you a shapely
new snack that looks like a
bugle. A crunchy little horn...
that tastes like corn!

Popsicle®

Carnation ice cream is so plain good ...it's good plain!

Carnation was the premiere ice cream of '66; it was even featured at Disneyland. Two favorite flavors I remember fondly are fudge ripple and peppermint stick. Carnation Ice Cream also made chocolate-coated vanilla ice cream bars with crunchies on them called "Kid Bars." Mrs. Donohue, the surly playground supervisor, would sell them on our way out of school, trying to horn in on Don the Ice Cream Man's action. Don would always park his truck across the street from the school, and he had a big line every day at two-thirty. My favorite after-school item was the banana taffy with the white racing stripe down the middle.

Popsicles were also a favorite purchase for me from Don the Ice Cream Man. My favorite flavor was root beer. The Popsicle company also made Fudgesicles and the timeless 50/50 Bar, sometimes called the Dreamsicle or Creamsicle. Make no mistake about it—this orange Popsicle filled with vanilla ice milk is one of the all-time classic dessert treats. Even the prestigious Häagen-Dazs company added this combo to their designer ice cream line. Another favorite was the rocket-shaped Popsicle.

Don continued to stop his truck at Encino Park up until the mid 1990s. In 1992, when I organized a reunion of my sixth grade class at Hesby Street School, Don parked his truck there and passed out ice cream bars to my stunned classmates—twenty years later.

New SIP'N CHIPS can radically change America's snack habits.

Here's how!

1
SIP'N CHIPS were made to go beautifully with beverages. (Or were beverages made for SIP'N CHIPS?)

2
Thin. Light. Mellow cheese flavor in each and every one. The better to eat by the handful.

3
They come in four amusing shapes. Designed to fit the curve of your hand.

4
Lightweight power to hold up to 10 times their weight in dips. No crumbling like old-time chips.

© NABISCO 1966

NEW OREO

GOOD THINGS LIKE CREAMIER FILLING MAKE THEM BEST!

TAKE ONE, BREAK ONE AND SEE!

See the lavish, creamy filling. Next—taste the most chocolate-y flavor ever in the crisp cookies. Discover why New Oreo is America's favorite chocolate sandwich cookie. The only one to buy!

OREO CREME SANDWICH

WHATEVER KINDS OF COOKIES YOU LIKE ... NABISCO BAKES THEM BETTER

Although I preferred Hydrox, Oreos were a lunchbox staple.

Jolly Time popcorn was the closest thing to movie popcorn. I remember the big silver pot my mom would use to prepare it, just in time for *Walt Disney's Wonderful World of Color* (which, in 1966, I still had to watch on a black-and-white TV).

POPPIN' FUN FOR THE WHOLE FAMILY!

JOLLY TIME POP CORN

from a Southern
Heirloom
Recipe
Sophie Mae
Peanut Brittle

Only Sophie Mae Peanut
Brittle is so thin, so
crisp, so full of peanuts.
Buy a box today at
your favorite grocery,
drug or variety store.

*Also available as a
delicious candy bar.*

SOPHIE MAE CANDY
of Atlanta, Georgia

Come take a trip through the
WRIGLEY ZOO where the
animals pop right up for you!

Around this time, the Jell-O
Company introduced instant Jell-O
for kids, which you would make by
simply adding water and allowing to
chill. The flavors were unique—
Candycorn Orange, Gumdrop
Grape—but, like Fizzies, they
contained artificial sweeteners found
to be dangerous (cyclamates) and
were quickly taken off the market.

This ad for Wrigley's gum ran in *Jack and
Jill* magazine. Their chewing gum was an
absolute necessity on family car trips. The
three flavors, Spearmint, Doublemint, and
Juicy Fruit, taste the same today. (Although
I still haven't figured out what the
predominant fruit flavor in Juicy Fruit is
supposed to be.)

WHOLE PURPLE PLUMS

DARK SWEET CHERRIES

YELLOW CLING SLICED PEACHES

A wonderful alternative to Bosco and Nestle's Quik, Clanky the space-age robot was a plastic figure worth keeping long after the syrup was squeezed out of him. This product originated in 1963 and was becoming hard to find by '66. I remember purchasing Clanky in his final days at Thrifty drug store. Along with Krazy Foam, Clanky became a favorite bathtub toy.

CLANKY CHOCOLATE FLAVOR SYRUP

Dad insisted on healthy desserts once in a while; they usually took the form of sugar-coated canned fruit from Del Monte. I liked Geisha brand mandarin oranges, which I actually thought were imported from Japan.

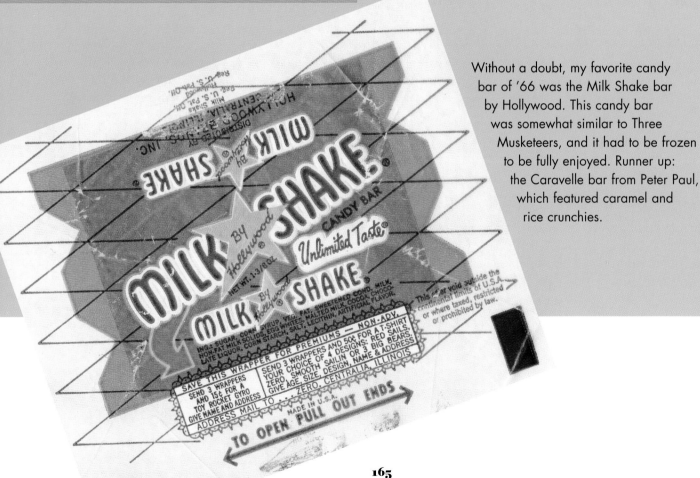

Without a doubt, my favorite candy bar of '66 was the Milk Shake bar by Hollywood. This candy bar was somewhat similar to Three Musketeers, and it had to be frozen to be fully enjoyed. Runner up: the Caravelle bar from Peter Paul, which featured caramel and rice crunchies.

In 1966, I found the selection of beverages absolutely overwhelming. Many of these effervescent classics still remain on the shelves today, like Fresca, Sprite, and Bubble Up. (Would someone at Canada Dry please honor my repeated requests to put "Wink" back on the market?) Probably the most common place for me to purchase these sodas in '66 was at one of the neighborhood gas stations, out of vending machines that had racks on the side where you would put the empty bottles.

Kool-Aid was the premier powdered drink mix of 1966. Pillsbury's Funny Face line was very popular, too, because of zany characters like Goofy Grape, Freckle Face Strawberry, Choo Choo Cherry, and Jolly Olly Orange.

I have to admit, there's nothing like drinking soda out of a glass bottle. If you doubt my word, pick up a six-pack of Orange Crush, Vernor's Ginger Ale, or A & W Root Beer (still available in glass-bottle six-packs), throw a few in some crushed ice, then pop one open and savor a few gulps. Are you not transported back to the halcyon days of summer in '66, listening to "Love Is Like an Itching in My Heart" or "Wild Thing" on your transistor radio?

Here's a toast to 1966 and the wonderful, delicious, and memorable food and drink it provided me with. And thank God my parents saved the Kool-Aid pitcher all these years! Now if Mom had only hung onto my Santa Claus mug with the candy-cane handle . . .

1 crazy calorie.

Unsticky. Unstuffy. Uninhibited. The Now Taste of Tab. Not so sweet.
With 1 crazy calorie in 6 ounces. It's what's helping so many people to keep slim and trim.
Tab. That's what's happening. To the nicest shapes around.

THE ONLY SOFT DRINK THAT DOESN'T TREAT YOU LIKE A KID.

You can't quench a thirst with a soft drink that tastes syrupy sweet.

Canada Dry Ginger Ale cuts through your thirst with the tart taste of ginger. It's pale dry. Light as it looks. Alive with tingling, refreshing bubbles.

Your thirst won't be back for a long while. Canada Dry wouldn't kid you.

Ice-cold Coca-Cola has the taste you never get tired of. Always refreshing. That's why things go better with Coke after Coke after Coke.

So there was this swingin' affair. And they drank a lot of Coca-Cola. Naturally. Because things go better with Coke after Coke after Coke. It has the taste you never get tired of.

The sassy one from Canada Dry.

Smooth but sassy, Wink is really hip.

One sip and you'll flip for Wink.

Crisp citrus flavor really cuts thirst in a Wink. You can even see the bits of fruit in the bottle.

Anytime your thirst tells you to drink, stop for a Wink.

COME ALIVE! You're in the Pepsi generation!

Pepsi-Cola cold beats any cola cold!

Drink Pepsi cold—the colder the better. Pepsi-Cola's taste was created for the cold. That special Pepsi taste comes alive in the cold. Drenching, quenching taste that never gives out before your thirst gives in. Pepsi pours it on!

Taste that beats the others cold... Pepsi pours it on!

"MATCHBOX"

SHOW CASE

MFD. by IDEAL TOY CORP. under license from LESNEY PRODUCTS & CO. LTD.
© 1966 LESNEY PRODUCTS AND CO. LTD.

How to tell a Marlin '66 from any other sports fastback.

FORD

1966

FAIRLANE

8
ON THE GO

In 1966, my neighborhood was home to a dazzling assortment of automobiles that exemplified the creative, innovative designs produced by auto manufacturers throughout the decade. I remember our family cars from that year—our yellow '66 Chevy Impala, and our powder blue Country Squire station wagon, which was actually a used '63 model that my dad bought at Ralph Williams Ford in Encino. (Ralph Williams was one of the preeminent car salesmen seen on local TV in Los Angeles throughout the '60s.)

My earliest mode of transportation was my beloved Schwinn Sting-Ray bike. I managed to traverse the entire neighborhood on my bike, and I still enjoy riding through it today on my fully restored lime green Sting-Ray. My next-door neighbor in '66 "Big Dave" Cohen was a few years older than I, and he had a candy-apple red Sting-Ray. As if his bike were a motorcycle, Dave would ride what seemed like an endless number of miles around the Valley, wearing his standard outfit: Birmingham High School gym shorts and white T-shirt. I will never forget one summer afternoon in the mid '60s when Dave's Sting-Ray actually broke in half from excessive use, and the Schwinn company granted him a brand new bike for free!

Schwinn Sting-Rays, which first became available in late 1963, were extremely popular throughout the decade, but they really hit a peak in popularity in 1966. One model even had a stick-shift gear changer patterned after actual hot-rod cars; another model I remember quite well was the "Ram's Horn," which had curved handlebars like a British racing bike, on a standard Sting-Ray frame with larger, thinner tires.

Here's my classic 1965 "flamboyant lime" Sting-Ray restored to exact original specifications, in front of my parents' home in Encino, 2002. The back wheel on the bike has one of the very cool treadless "Slik" tires that were so popular on Sting-Rays in the '60s. This created a "dragster" feel on the road to school.

This is a fully restored candy-apple red Sting-Ray like my neighbor Dave popped his wheelies on. When approaching his house, Dave would fly down the street at light speed, and take a really wide turn into his parents' driveway. He would then skid to a stop . . . with the back wheel sliding around in a perfect arc. (Note how similar my parents' home looks today to how it did in '66!)

In 1966 Schwinn bikes tied in their catalog and advertising with Disneyland. This ad is from the back of a *Lois Lane* comic book.

I remember seeing quite a bit of these motor scooters and heavy-duty motorcycles in the neighborhood. One of the hip teens on the block, Mike Kane, tooled around on his Yamaha sportbike, while several of the edgier teens had little minibikes, which my parents deemed much too dangerous for my brother and me. The principal manufacturer of these minibikes that I remember was a company called Taco. Only the rough kids had these supercharged sources of transportation, although the Yamaha sport cycles depicted here were popular with college kids.

In '66 I also began collecting Matchbox cars. These high-quality die-cast metal miniature autos were extremely detailed and well made. They were British imports (from a company called Lesney), which made them extremely classy. If I went for a whole week with good behavior (i.e., no pouring a whole box of Mr. Bubble in the tub) Mom would take me to Nahas department store and I would get to pick out a Matchbox car. My brother had a similar arrangement, which was predicated on him going the whole week without jumping into my parents' bed to sleep.

SOOTY SAM
Chaos at the Crossing

When Davey Said He Started Smoking
... It's Plain To See He Wasn't Joking!

WADE DOES 150 ON THE STRAIGHTS . . .
WHEN HE DISQUALIFIES DRIVERS HE HATES !

Another fond transportation memory: my Weird-Oh's trading cards, which featured wacky dragster characters reminiscent of Big Daddy Roth's Rat Fink.

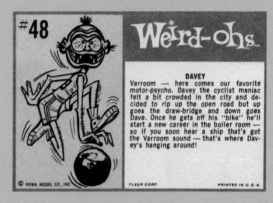

#48

Weird-ohs

DAVEY
Varroom — here comes our favorite motor-psycho. Davey the cyclist maniac felt a bit crowded in the city and decided to rip up the open road but up goes the draw-bridge and down goes Dave. Once he gets off his "bike" he'll start a new career in the boiler room — so if you soon hear a ship that's got the Varroom sound — that's where Davey's hanging around!

© HAWK MODEL CO., INC. FLEER CORP. PRINTED IN U.S.A.

MINIATURE CARS CARRYING CASE

Mattel Toys attempted to cash in on the '66 Matchbox car craze with this carrying case that fit the British Matchbox cars, and later with the Mattel Hot Wheels cars.

Ride with Lloyd Bridges through "The Wonderful World of Wheels"

Thurs., Sept. 8, 7:30 EDT, CBS-TV
Sponsored by Du Pont ZEREX

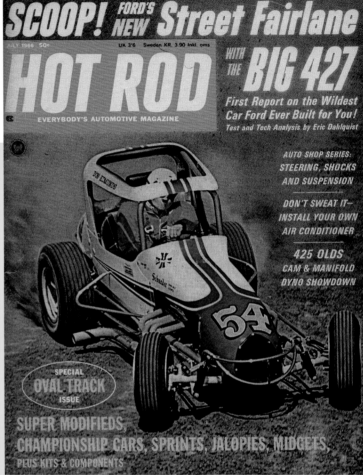

Sweetheart of the Supermarket Set

It had to be. With non-stop thrift, with extra-nimble performance, with all-around, All-American elegance, Mustang has become the sweetheart of the Supermarket Set.

They like the way it makes sense with gas. More miles per gallon is about the heart of it. They relish the way Mustang maneuvers into tight parking spots, the good performance of the 200-cubic-inch Six on the open road.

And Mustang makes people feel just great. Great at the supermarket . . . grand at the opera . . . casually elegant everywhere. (Why not, with bucket seats, snappy stick shift, plush carpeting and all the other no-cost specials that a Mustang features?)

Why not make a date for a test-drive? You, too, can go places with the sweetheart of the Supermarket Set!

MUSTANG
A PRODUCT OF Ford

Many American cars of 1966 derived their sporty design from the hot-rod world. This gave the suburban middle-class family the opportunity to show off some European prestige and capture a youthful appearance. Although American cars continued to develop their sporty profile in the later '60s, 1966 was a transitional year in which the Ford Mustang (originally released in late 1964) really became the standard for the neighborhood sports-car enthusiast.

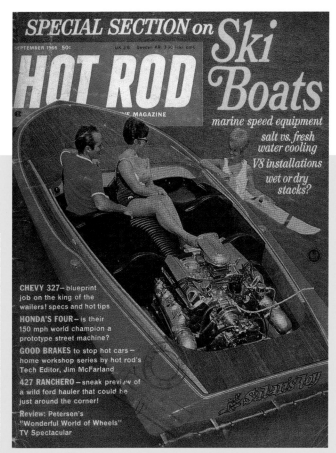

SPECIAL SECTION on *Ski Boats*

SEPTEMBER 1966 50c

UK 3/6 Sweden KR 3.90 (inkl. oms)

HOT ROD
THE MAGAZINE

marine speed equipment
salt vs. fresh water cooling
V8 installations
wet or dry stacks?

CHEVY 327—blueprint job on the king of the wailers! specs and hot tips

HONDA'S FOUR—is their 150 mph world champion a prototype street machine?

GOOD BRAKES to stop hot cars—home workshop series by hot rod's Tech Editor, Jim McFarland

427 RANCHERO—sneak preview of a wild ford hauler that could be just around the corner!

Review: Petersen's "Wonderful World of Wheels" TV Spectacular

MAY DRAGMATE

Photo: Universal Studios

CHEVROLET

The ultimate '66 sports car: the Chevrolet Corvette. Years later, it's still a classic.

George Barris's Kustom Dragster, as seen in the teen film *Out of Sight*. (Hood ornament optional.)

Classic cool: the 1966 Dodge Charger awarded to *Playboy* Playmate of the Year Allison Parks.

Even though you dearly love your fastback Barracuda, you still don't need the most expensive motor oil.

Just the best.

You're probably one of those guys who lavishes attention on a car. Especially the engine. Well, we feel the same way about motor oil. Using tests established by auto makers, we constantly check Gulfpride® Single-G for its ability to protect against wear, scuffing, rusting, deposit formation and clogging.

Gulfpride far surpasses the requirements of car makers in these tests. Recent competitive tests show Gulfpride Single-G performance equals or exceeds that of four leading competitive premium motor oils. (And one of them costs 25¢ a quart more than Gulfpride.)

Get the best protection for your engine. Get Gulfpride wherever you see the Sign of the Gulf Orange Disc.

Gulf

GULF OIL CORPORATION

Tired of compacts that put you too close for comfort? Arms too close to the door . . . legs too close to the floor? Think big, think smart. Get fired up with the new '66 Dodge Dart GT. With Dart GT, you can insist on size and still economize. Check the price. Check the interior: foam-padded seats, wall-to-wall carpeting, door-to-door luxury. Demand more comfort in your compact—more spirit, more for your money. Step into '66 Dart. Take it on the road. Which way do you want to go, Six or V8? '66 Dodge Dart goes both ways without attacking your budget. If you're fed up with compacts that don't make it in size, styling, and spunk, you've got it made with '66 Dart. The Dodge-sized compact. It's got what you want. The Dodge Rebellion wants you.

'66 Dodge Dart

DODGE DIVISION  CHRYSLER MOTORS CORPORATION

JOIN THE DODGE REBELLION

Avoid the cramped compact squeeze.

Stretch out in '66 Dodge Dart.

Fast new version of the car that got America thinking fastback. '66 Barracuda.

The 1966 AMC Barracuda. Our neighbors across the street had one exactly like this, and I remember thinking how cool it was when the engine would rev up and Mr. Baken would peel out of the driveway on his way up to the Piggly Wiggly or Orange Julius to pick up a couple of chili dogs.

Internationally hip Fiat convertible with underwater diver chick reminiscent of Bond girl Claudine Auger in *Thunderball*.

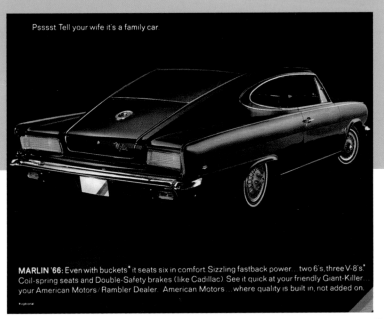

The legendary 1966 Chrysler Imperial. This was the car used to make the Green Hornet's Black Beauty supercar seen on TV this year.

Even the more conservative vehicles of this year took on a flashier, mod look that gave businessmen and housewives the opportunity to achieve high style while driving to the office, going to the supermarket, picking up the babysitter, or taking a family road trip. In my family these trips were usually to Disneyland, Vacation Village in San Diego, or Palm Springs.

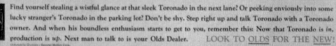

In the late '80s I purchased a '66 black Imperial Crown Coupe, which I have fully restored. I only drive it on rare occasions, because most parking spaces today don't accommodate this mammoth but incredibly well designed vehicle. What a spectacular feeling for me to travel about in the same car in which Kato chauffeured the Green Hornet! One day, I may take my Imperial to custom car designer Dean Jeffries, who built the Black Beauty, and have him make me one.

There were so many memorable filling stations in 1966 . . . Gulf, Phillips 66, Flying A, Richfield, Union 76, and Texaco. There were always great soda vending machines at these stations where I remember drinking Bubble Up and Hires Root Beer during the hot San Fernando Valley summers. I also remember going up to the corner Gulf station to fill my Sting-Ray tires with air, and during this year they were giving away gold-tinted drinking glasses with antique cars on them . . . our neighbors, the Cohens, had a complete set from which I used to drink Hawaiian Punch and Kool-Aid.

Even though you paid $1,200 to restore this '57 T-Bird, you still don't need the most expensive motor oil.

Just the best.

Most people can get awfully hung up on taking care of a car like this. Especially the engine.

And that's where our motor oil comes in.

Using tests established by auto makers, we constantly check Gulfpride® Single-G for its ability to protect against wear, scuffing, rusting, deposit formation and clogging.

Gulfpride far surpasses the requirements of car makers in these tests. Recent competitive tests show Gulfpride Single-G performance equals or exceeds that of four leading competitive premium motor oils. (And one of them costs 25¢ a quart more than Gulfpride.) Get the best protection for your engine. Get Gulfpride wherever you see the Sign of the Gulf Orange Disc.

GULF OIL CORPORATION

When I was in first grade in '66, I remember reading about the far-off future of the 1980s, when we would all live in bubble houses and ride to work on a monorail—similar to the one at Disneyland, seen here along with the futuristic Flying Saucers. The Flying Saucers (powered by air jets) were at the park for the last year during '66. I only got to ride them one time, but will always remember the thrill of feeling like Elroy Jetson on his way to school. Ironically, over the decades many of the futuristic designs of '60s automobiles have become classics.

Other than a flying saucer, the classiest form of air travel in '66 was undoubtedly the magnificent Pan Am jet airplane. I still have a 1966 Pan Am flight bag, and I'll always remember John Lennon exiting the plane at Kennedy airport in early '64 toting his Pan Am bag as well. Pan Am was the airline of choice for both Frank Sinatra and James Bond, proof that there was no better way to jet-set around the globe.

The road to the future was paved with many happy memories of a special era in automotive design. For me, the thrill of transportation in '66 meant riding with my mom on weekend errands to the Children's Bootery shoe store . . . or even taking a long drive with my family to someplace like Chinatown or Ship's Coffee Shop in West Los Angeles. I was safe in the backseat with my brother Bobby and newborn sister Byrdie, envisioning my dad and mom as the pilot and co-pilot of our family's spacecraft, taking us to various galaxies along the Ventura and Hollywood freeways.

SAMMY DAVIS

Sears

Sears Has Everything

GE

GUARANTEED *Blue*
flashcubes
FOUR FLASHES IN ONE!

1966
PLAYBOY

PLAYMATE CALENDAR
75¢

9
FACES&PLACES

In 1966, I was a young boy with an impressionable mind and an indomitable imagination. It was in this year, for the first time in my life, that I really began to have heroes and fantasy figures. Later, in my work as a manager and in advertising, I would be fortunate enough to meet and develop professional alliances with many of my childhood idols, some of whom are featured in this chapter. The people and places of '66 have had an amazing, lasting influence on me—for over thirty-six years.

Now that we are nearing the end of our journey, I would like to dedicate this final chapter to the people and places that made 1966 a year I will never forget. I would also like to thank all of you who took the time to look through my scrapbook. I hope that it has been a happy journey, and that now we agree 1966 was, in fact, the coolest year in pop culture history.

The author and brother Bob, walking the plank at the Gene Autry Motel in Palm Springs, during the summer of '66.

Raquel Welch holding a very fortunate bottle of Dad's root beer. Classic soda pop backdrop in which images of Squirt, Dr. Pepper, Fresca, and Vernor's resonate.

Raquel, posing poolside in '66, displays the winning form that catapulted her to international stardom this year with her appearance in the sci-fi film *Fantastic Voyage*. Why couldn't my swim teacher have looked like this?

Raquel hitting one hundred strokes before bedtime.

Sultry sex kitten Deanna Lund, whom I first saw in 1965's *Dr. Goldfoot and the Bikini Machine*. She would be seen in the film *Tony Rome* with Frank Sinatra in '67, and would star in ABC's *Land of the Giants* from 1968 to 1970. (I always loved the "Jack and the Beanstalk" concept of that show.)

Jill St. John demonstrated a similar dance step on the premiere episode of *Batman*, as the Riddler's accomplice Molly. "You shake a pretty mean cape, Batman!" Molly exclaimed as she watched him debut the "Batusi" at the "What a Way to Go-Go." Here, Jill shakes a pretty mean beach towel.

Jill St. John was featured in the film *The Oscar* in 1966.

Nancy gives Raquel a run for her money in the white-bikini contest.

189

Adam West and Van Williams share crime-fighting tips at the press conference that introduced Williams as TV's new Green Hornet.

Adam West and Burt Ward defy gravity in rehearsal for a Batclimb sequence. Sammy Davis, Jr., reacts with amusement as Adam asks him to become a member of the "Bat Pack."

Bruce Lee—the ultimate martial arts icon.

William Dozier, executive producer of and mentor to both the *Batman* and the *Green Hornet* TV series on ABC. Dozier was a highly literate man who sought out top-notch writers to craft the *Batman* scripts, most notably Lorenzo Semple, Jr., who wrote the pilot and several other episodes.

Van Williams and Bruce Lee set their sights on a hit TV show with *The Green Hornet*. It only lasted a year on network TV but has been a favorite of mine ever since.

Neal Hefti, brilliant musical arranger. In 1966, Hefti composed the classic *Batman* theme, with which he charted as a hit single. The Marketts and the Ventures also had hit singles with their versions of the theme. In the early '60s, Hefti had worked with Frank Sinatra, arranging two of his best albums: *Sinatra and Basie* and *Sinatra and Swingin' Brass*. Hefti also composed many great film and TV scores including *Sex and the Single Girl*, *Barefoot in the Park*, and TV's *The Odd Couple*.

America's #1 in the sun.

Don't be a paleface!

Tan, don't burn, use Coppertone.®

JULIE NEWMAR...co-starring in "Mackenna's Gold," a Columbia Release

Coppertone gives you a better tan.

C'mon, join the tan-ables! Get the fastest tan with maximum protection. That darker, deeper, richer tan... skin that feels satiny soft, smooth. Let Coppertone give you a better tan! More people rely on its exclusive moisturizing-tanning formula than any other suntan product in the world.

Julie strikes a shimmering pose for Coppertone, with a swimsuit reminiscent of the outfits in the Bond film *Goldfinger*. Julie's statuesque physique and dancer's poise made her a formidable adversary for Batman and Robin. Here, Julie seems to be leaning more on her charm than her criminal instincts to steal the heart of this fortunate frogman.

Beverly Adams played Matt Helm's secretary Lovey Kravezit in the '66 films *The Silencers* and *Murderers' Row*. She proves here that three is not a crowd.

Stefanie Powers first came to my attention in reruns of the 1963 film *Palm Springs Weekend*. In 1966 Stefanie starred as April Dancer in *The Girl from U.N.C.L.E.*; with her subtle British accent, she was the perfect choice for the role. Here, she demonstrates the shing-a-ling dance for attentive surfers.

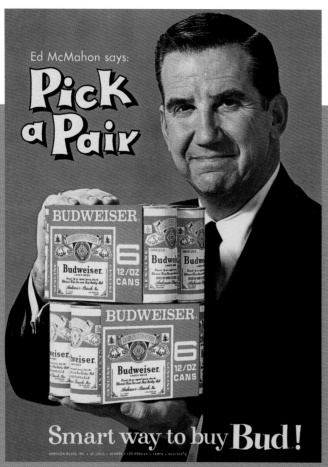
Ed McMahon begins a long-running campaign as pitch man for Budweiser.

Sean Connery, fresh off the success of *Thunderball*, pitches Jim Beam whiskey. He has always been a major hero figure for me, and I still marvel at his '60s Bond movies and his timeless appeal.

NOTED STARS WOODY ALLEN AND MONIQUE VAN VOOREN ENJOY THEIR SMIRNOFF MULES TOGETHER.

THIS IS THE DRINK THAT IS...THE SMIRNOFF MULE

Give a Mule party! You couldn't serve a smarter drink. For a cool, refreshing Mule made with Smirnoff and 7-Up® is a choice you can start with and stay with. Only crystal clear Smirnoff, filtered through 14,000 pounds of activated charcoal, blends so perfectly with 7-Up. So follow the rule when mixing the Mule. Make it with *Smirnoff!*

Smirnoff Mule Recipe
Jigger of Smirnoff over ice.
Add juice of ¼ lime. Fill Mule
mug or glass with 7-Up to
taste. Delicious.
Set of 6 Mule mugs—$3.00.
Send check or money order
payable to Smirnoff Mule,
Department H. P. O. Box 225,
B'klyn, N.Y. 11202

Always ask for *Smirnoff* VODKA   *It leaves you breathless®*

Woody Allen for Smirnoff
vodka. Woody based one of
his stand-up acts on his
experience posing with actress
Monique Van Vooren.

Josephine the Plumber (played
by Jane Withers) makes a
splash for Comet cleanser.

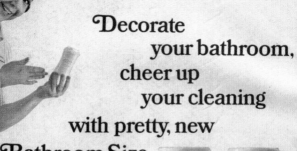

Decorate
your bathroom,
cheer up
your cleaning
with pretty, new
Bathroom Size
Comet,
it's all plastic!
Now,
the best cleanser
in the newest size
for easier cleaning!

"Now it's in plastic and Bathroom Size Comet is nicer than
ever," says Josephine, the Lady Plumber.
"Lovelier colors, smart new shape to decorate your bathroom.
When you leave one out your family may take
the hint and clean up now and then. This cute Comet sprinkles
easily in tight spots. And New Extra Strength
Comet cleans best, disinfects best. It's the stain-
removing cleanser with Super Chlorinol. Get new
Bathroom Size Comet in aqua,
pink or yellow plastic."

Four to a bundle

Nancy gives new meaning to the phrase "window dressing."

Tina Louise is best known for her portrayal of Ginger, the sultriest castaway on *Gilligan's Island*. But she was also a talented dramatic actress, with countless TV and film roles to her credit. In 1975 she would give a chilling performance as a too-perfect housewife in *The Stepford Wives*.

Brigitte Bardot was still a striking sex symbol in '66, and this famous pose was later recreated by supermodel Elle McPherson on a cover of *Playboy* magazine. Bardot was releasing pop records throughout the '60s as well as starring in offbeat European films. I fondly remember her from 1965's *Dear Brigitte*; I was jealous that Billy Mumy got to meet her instead of me.

Sharon Tate first broke through in 1966 in Roman Polanski's *The Fearless Vampire Killers*. In 1967, her stunning good looks would hit a soft spot with me in *Don't Make Waves* and in the camp classic *Valley of the Dolls*, in which she played ill-fated starlet Jennifer North.

Rising starlet Michele Carey, who would later star with Elvis in *Live a Little, Love a Little* (1968).

Deanna Lund didn't wait around much in '66. . . . She appeared in many films, including *Out of Sight*, *The Oscar*, *Spinout*, and *The Swinger*.

Wende Wagner, the Green Hornet's sizzling, seductive secretary, made a strong impression on my first-grade libido.

Fresh-faced British beauty Julie Christie coming off the success of 1965's *Darling*.

In '66, Barbra Streisand was already a powerful icon and highly gifted vocal talent.

Kitten with a whip, Ann-Margret, shows off her purrfect feline prowess. By '66 Ann had become a bona-fide sex symbol, with films like *Bye Bye Birdie* (1963) and *Viva Las Vegas* (1964) already under her belt. Later in the decade I would catch a rerun of her 1963 appearance as "Ann-Margrock" on *The Flintstones*—which would secure a permanent place for her in my personal "Hal of Fame."

Marlo Thomas debuted as struggling actress Ann Marie on the wonderfully whimsical ABC series *That Girl*. Marlo's sparkling personality and adorably scratchy voice made an indelible impression on me.

Marlo Thomas.

Marlo admits that her new series closely parallels her own amazing success story.

< This Girl Is... "THAT GIRL" >

GOLD KEY

30040-001 JANUARY

BONUS: GIANT BUFFY POSTER INSIDE!   25¢

Family Affair

It shines with humor —it glows with warmth!

Kathy Garver, *Family Affair*'s unforgettable Cissy, one of the sweetest TV teens of '66. She had that "Pan Am stewardess" thing about her.

Elizabeth Montgomery as seen in the '66 TV season of *Bewitched*. Samantha Stephens was a character I was instantly attracted to. She had a wonderful blend of maternal warmth and sublime sex appeal. And that mischievous twitch knocked me out!

Lesley Ann Warren was the quintessential Cinderella in the Rodgers and Hammerstein TV musical, which first aired in 1965. (It was rerun throughout the '60s and into the '70s.) I will always remember the believability she brought to the role, the storybook charm of the set design, and her heart-breaking performance of "In My Own Little Corner."

Hugh Hefner conducts one of his many informal interviews at the Chicago headquarters of *Playboy* magazine. In the late '60s, when he began hosting the TV show *Playboy after Dark*, Hefner would open a new *Playboy* office on the Sunset Strip, complete with his own penthouse apartment. I always got a kick out of seeing the rabbit-head logo on the side of the building.

Barbara Eden and Larry Hagman star as Jeannie and Major Nelson in the second season of one of the many classic fantasy sitcoms of the 1960s. I got my finger stuck in one of my dad's liquor bottles trying to pull out a genie of my own.

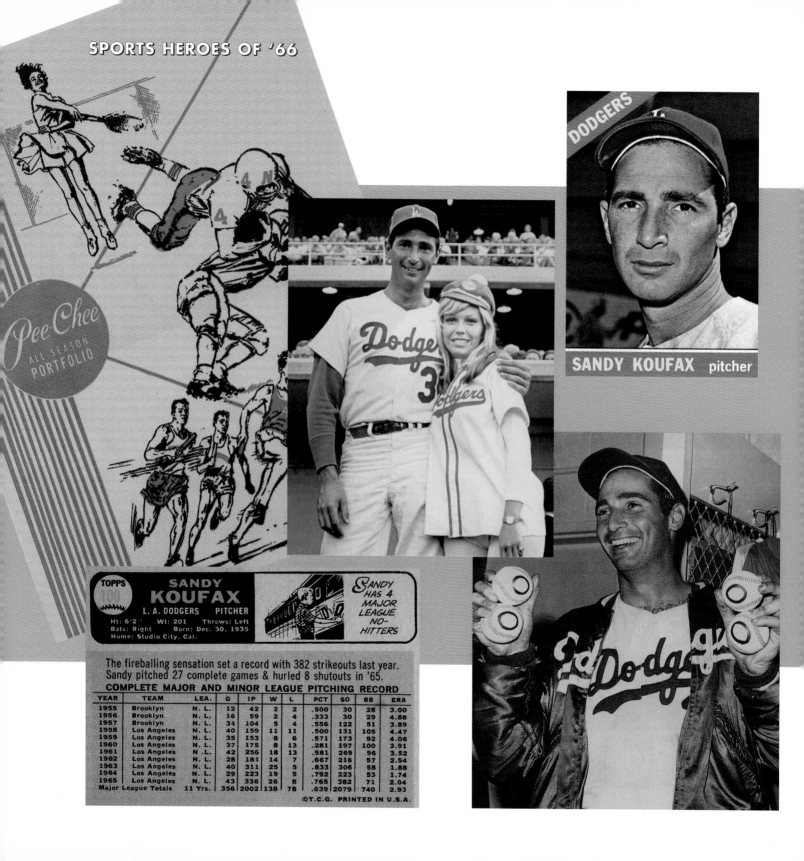

Pee-Chee
ALL SEASON
PORTFOLIO

DODGERS

SANDY KOUFAX   pitcher

TOPPS 100   SANDY
KOUFAX
L. A. DODGERS   PITCHER
Ht: 6'2"   Wt: 201   Throws: Left
Bats: Right   Born: Dec. 30, 1935
Home: Studio City, Cal.

SANDY
HAS 4
MAJOR
LEAGUE
NO-
HITTERS

The fireballing sensation set a record with 382 strikeouts last year.
Sandy pitched 27 complete games & hurled 8 shutouts in '65.

COMPLETE MAJOR AND MINOR LEAGUE PITCHING RECORD

YEAR	TEAM	LEA.	G	IP	W	L	PCT	SO	BB	ERA
1955	Brooklyn	N. L.	12	42	2	2	.500	30	28	3.00
1956	Brooklyn	N. L.	16	59	2	4	.333	30	29	4.88
1957	Brooklyn	N. L.	34	104	5	4	.556	122	51	3.89
1958	Los Angeles	N. L.	40	159	11	11	.500	131	105	4.47
1959	Los Angeles	N. L.	35	153	8	6	.571	173	92	4.06
1960	Los Angeles	N. L.	37	175	8	13	.281	197	100	3.91
1961	Los Angeles	N. L.	42	256	18	13	.581	269	96	3.52
1962	Los Angeles	N. L.	28	181	14	7	.667	216	57	2.54
1963	Los Angeles	N. L.	40	311	25	5	.833	306	58	1.88
1964	Los Angeles	N. L.	29	223	19	5	.792	223	53	1.74
1965	Los Angeles	N. L.	43	336	26	8	.765	382	71	2.04
Major League Totals	11 Yrs.		356	2002	138	78	.639	2079	740	2.93

©T.C.G. PRINTED IN U.S.A.

Sandy Koufax is my number one all-time sports hero. He was a dynamic, awesome presence on the mound at Dodger Stadium in the '60s. I will never forget seeing him pitch in the first World Series I remember watching, which was 1965. The Dodgers won against the Minnesota Twins. The next season (1966) would be Sandy's last on the mound, as he would succumb to chronic arthritis in his left elbow. I will always remember him not just as the greatest baseball pitcher of all time, but also as a man of great character and personal morals.

Sandy refused to pitch on Yom Kippur, the holiest of Jewish holidays, even while the Dodgers were in the World Series. In '66 Sandy and fellow superstar pitcher Don Drysdale made a landmark salary deal (over one hundred thousand dollars each for the year) as a dynamic-duo pitching team. Don Drysdale continued to pitch for three more years and retired in 1969. I remember in the San Fernando Valley there was a nightclub called "Don Drysdale's Dugout" that I always wanted to go to, but by the time I would have been old enough to gain entrance in 1981, it was gone.

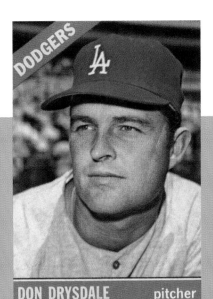

DON DRYSDALE   pitcher

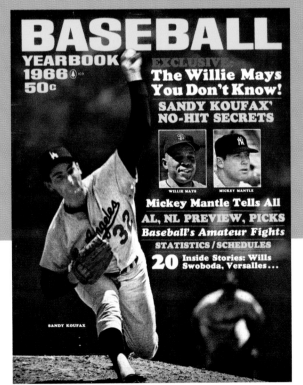

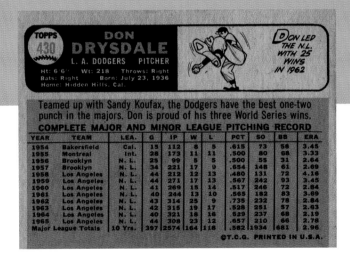

TRADING FACES

RED SOX · **CARL YASTRZEMSKI** outfield

PIRATES · **WILLIE STARGELL** outfield

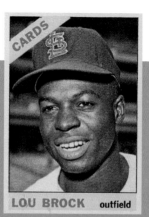

CARDS · **LOU BROCK** outfield

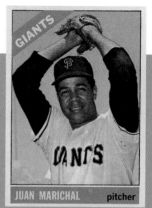

GIANTS · **JUAN MARICHAL** pitcher

GIANTS · **WILLIE MAYS** outfield

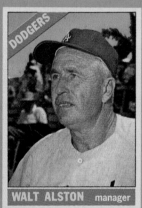

DODGERS · **WALT ALSTON** manager

DODGERS · **JIM BREWER** pitcher

DODGERS · **NICK WILLHITE** pitcher

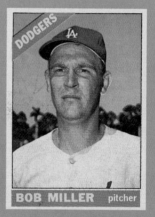

DODGERS · **BOB MILLER** pitcher

DODGERS · **JOHN KENNEDY** 3rd base

DODGERS · **HECTOR VALLE** catcher

DODGERS · **RON FAIRLY** outfield

DODGERS · **JOHN ROSEBORO** catcher

ANGELS · **JIM FREGOSI** shortstop

ANGELS · **ALBIE PEARSON** outfield

WILLIE HORTON outfield

FRED GLADDING pitcher

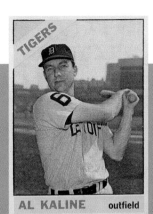

AL KALINE outfield

BERT CAMPANERIS shortstop

TONY PEREZ 1st base

RON MIX TACKLE SAN DIEGO CHARGERS

CHUCK ALLEN LINEBACKER SAN DIEGO CHARGERS

WALT SWEENEY GUARD SAN DIEGO CHARGERS

STEW BARBER TACKLE BUFFALO BILLS

SAM DeLUCA GUARD NEW YORK JETS

JIM TURNER KICKER NEW YORK JETS

DICK WOOD QUARTERBACK MIAMI DOLPHINS

DICK WESTMORELAND DEFENSIVE BACK MIAMI DOLPHINS

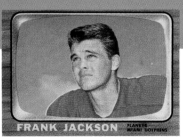

FRANK JACKSON FLANKER MIAMI DOLPHINS

MICKEY SLAUGHTER QUARTERBACK DENVER BRONCOS

The great Willie Mays.

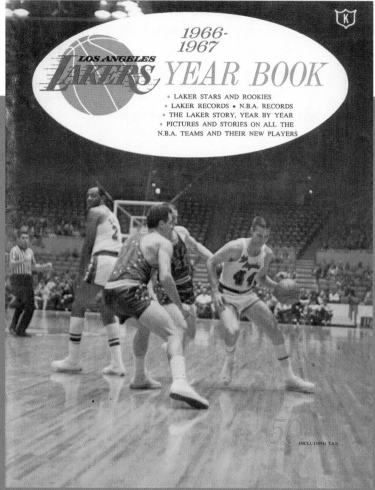

Nineteen sixty-six L.A. Dodgers yearbook. Although the Dodgers lost the World Series this year, I still enjoyed eating peanuts and Dodger Dogs at Dodger Stadium with my dad and brother Bob. It was in this year that I became determined to enlist in our neighborhood Little League, mostly for the cool uniform.

Nineteen sixty-six Lakers yearbook featuring "Mr. Clutch" Jerry West and Elgin Baylor. Both these men would defy gravity with their never-ending "hang in the air" lay-ups. My neighbor Sparky Rifkin did a pretty impressive imitation of Baylor's "around the back" lay-up.

Jim Ryun breaks the outdoor world record for the mile. This event kick-started my lifelong passion for long-distance running. (My dad also began jogging around the block with his buddy Sid Cohen this year.)

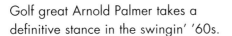

Golf great Arnold Palmer takes a definitive stance in the swingin' '60s.

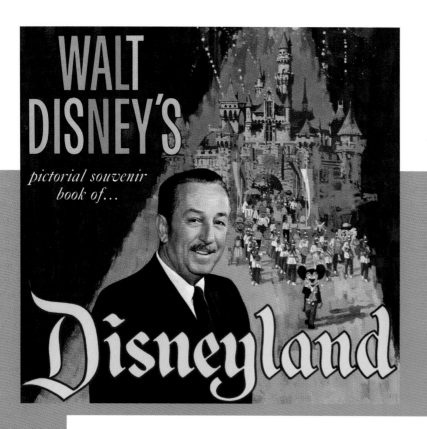

WALT DISNEY'S

pictorial souvenir book of...

Disneyland

I have so many wonderful memories of going to Disneyland from throughout the '60s, but 1966 was a particularly great year to visit the Magic Kingdom. This was the first year I stayed at the Disneyland Hotel and rode the monorail into the Park. What a thrill! I got to ride the Flying Saucers for the first (and final) time. I saw all the wondrous, colorful images and the imagination that emanated from Uncle Walt's vision of a real-life utopia.

I remember drinking orange juice at the Sunkist Citrus House on Main Street and, of course, the magical Tiki punch which was sold in front of the Enchanted Tiki Room. If I was on my best behavior, we would go for dinner at the Tahitian Terrace restaurant, where live hula girls performed.

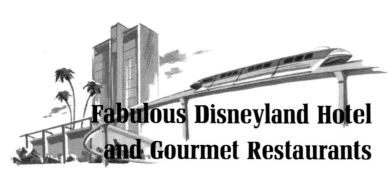

Fabulous Disneyland Hotel and Gourmet Restaurants

Vacation and recreation center for all Southern California is the Anaheim area—Disneyland's "home city." And the "official hotel" at the Magic Kingdom is the exciting Disneyland Hotel.

Located directly across the street from Disneyland Park —and connected directly to Tomorrowland via monorail trains—the Disneyland Hotel is a year 'round resort, designed and priced for family fun.

Disney's vision of the future was embodied in Tomorrowland, where the bandstand rose from the ground and the architecture featured a *Jetsons*-like motif. I remember reading in my schoolbook how, in the future, cities would all have space architecture and monorail systems. "The future" was supposed to be a reality by around the 1980s. It all hasn't happened— but much of the high-tech gadgetry that came into use in the year 1966 has evolved tremendously since then.

Tomorrowland's House of the Future, made of plastic

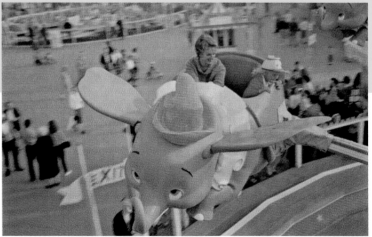

Disneyland was the first theme park in which computers assisted in the presentation of the attractions. The Enchanted Tiki Room, the Jungle Cruise, and Great Moments with Mr. Lincoln were the first attractions to implement audio-animatronic robots.

In 1966, Disneyland was eleven years old and still very much in its "innocent phase." Corporate sponsors were present, as in the Carnation Ice Cream parlor on Main Street (still there), but it was subtle.

Today, many of my favorite attractions from the glory days have vanished, like Skull Rock, the Submarines, and the Skyway buckets that rode through the Matterhorn, but the park is still a wonderful, nostalgic place for my friends and me to visit. When I ride the train around the park, I become a kid again. It is like the "Kick the Can" episode of *The Twilight Zone*. Childhood will always reign supreme at Disneyland!

Sadly, on December 15, 1966, Uncle Walt passed away, but his genius and progressive concepts live on.

Snow White & the Seven Dwarfs are often seen in Fantasyland.

The Oceanarium at Marineland of the Pacific

Marineland was a fabulous aquatic theme park in Palos Verdes, California. I loved going there to see Bubbles the whale and the dolphin shows, and when looking through the glass of the huge aquariums I felt like I was watching an episode of *Diver Dan* or *Sea Hunt*.

I would always see this ad for Palisades Amusement Park while reading my DC comic books. I always wanted to see the place, but I couldn't convince my parents to drive to New Jersey. The park was immortalized in Freddy Cannon's song "Palisades Park" a few years earlier (1962). Interesting trivia note: the song was written by TV game show producer and host Chuck Barris.

Santa's Village in California's San Bernardino Mountains presented a fantastic real-life view of Santa and his industrious elves. It was an unforgettable field trip destination for my Cub Scout troop and me; I got to pet real reindeer and take home a pair of little elf slippers. After Candy Cane Lane in Woodland Hills, this was the ultimate holiday spectacle.

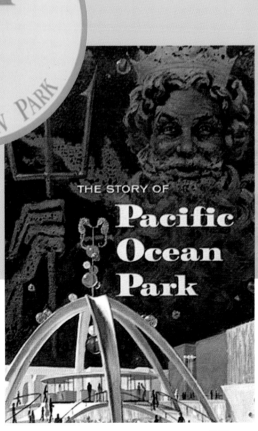

THE STORY OF
Pacific Ocean Park

The magnificent Pacific Ocean Park was a fascinating, colorful place to visit in 1966, its final full year of operation. I vividly remember the giant, majestic statue of King Neptune that greeted visitors at the entrance. It was used in many '60s movies and TV shows, like the touching episode of *The Twilight Zone* "In Praise of Pip" (1963), in which Jack Klugman chases his son through the funhouse.

Here are some of the most important places my family and I visited in 1966, right in our own neighborhood. Dinner at Du-Par's for chicken pot pies, and Sunday brunch at the International House of Pancakes. I still eat at Barone's (rectangular pizza even Sinatra approved of!) and Casa Vega (where Jack Nicholson and Marlon Brando would hang out). Circus Liquor was a great place to buy baseball cards and Caravelle candy bars. (Their sign would be featured in the film *Clueless*.) There were weekend visits to Sears, Kentucky Fried Chicken, and Thrifty Drug (featuring five cent ice cream cones served with a cylindrical scooper).

During the summer of '66, Baskin-Robbins in Encino was a frequent pit stop. My favorite flavor was Beatle Nut, and the root beer floats were great, too. (The root beer was in a big wooden barrel.) We would sit in little school desks, and there was a dairy-farm mural on the wall. Summer attire was purchased at Hawaii of the Valley.

The Encino Bowl was a popular hangout for me. Great crinkle-cut French fries in red plastic baskets . . . and pinball machines. (The resident "pro" on the premises was Foy Belcher.) I always wanted my own bowling ball, but I had to settle for a little rosin bag with which to dry my hands out of a vending machine. The "alternate" bowling alley was the Corbin Bowl in nearby Tarzana. I attended many terrific birthday parties at these Ventura Boulevard establishments.

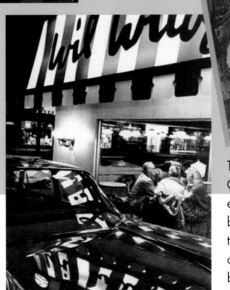

The best coffee shop I ever patronized was Ships, where you could make your own toast at the table. All three Ships were in the L.A. area (not the Valley) so it was a special treat to go there. Ships was built using '50s astrospace design, known as "Googie" architecture. (The Hughes Market sign had a similar rocket-ship motif.) Bob's Big Boy drive-in on Van Nuys Boulevard was another fun place to eat, and I loved the free Big Boy comics they gave out.

The Lifson family residence since May 1963. Other than going to Wil Wright's (the expensive ice cream parlor) for a deluxe butterscotch sundae, this was my favorite place to be in 1966. I would ride up the driveway on my Sting-Ray and dash inside to my bedroom just to the right of the front door. There's no place like home!

PHOTO CREDITS

ABKCO Music, Inc.

Archie Comics, Inc.

Kevin Burns

Capitol Records, Inc.

Bruce Clark

Condé Nast Publications, Inc.

DC Comics

EMI Group plc

Fox Entertainment Group, Inc.

Cindy Gold

Hal Lifson Photo Archive

Harvey Comics, Inc.

Hearst Communications, Inc.

Jean Cummings Photo Archive

Mark London

Metro-Goldwyn-Mayer, Inc.

Paramount Pictures Corporation

Playboy Enterprises, Inc.

Random House

Joe Russo

Nancy Sinatra

Sony Music Entertainment, Inc.

Shaune Steele

Time, Inc.

TV Guide, Inc.

Universal Music Group

The Walt Disney Company

Warner Music Group

Lesley Ann Warren

Fred Wostbrock

Williams a·go·go

4 PLAYER FLIPPER GAME

FEATURING

NEW CAPTIVE BALL SPINNER UNIT

SCORING VALUES

1. EXTRA BALL PLUS 200
2. COLLECT BONUS (100 UP TO 1900)
3. 500 POINTS OR 50 POINTS

HIGH SCORE SKILL LANE (UP TO TOP OF PLAYFIELD). 4 HIGH POWERED FLIPPERS. WIDE OPEN ACTION PACKED PLAYFIELD.

- STANDARD 3 WAY MULTIPLE CHUTE
- STAINLESS STEEL MOULDING & TRIM
- NUMBER MATCH
- 3 OR 5 BALL PLAY
- AUTOMATIC BALL LIFT

Williams ELECTRONIC MANUFACTURING CORP.
3401 North California Ave.   Chicago, Illinois 60618 • Cable address: WILCOIN, CHICAGO
AVAILABLE FOR IMMEDIATE DELIVERY THROUGH YOUR WILLIAMS DISTRIBUTOR